I0470889

First Impressions for the Business Professional

Why Some of Us Excel and Most of Us Fail

First Impressions for the Business Professional

Why Some of Us Excel and Most of Us Fail

By

Christopher J. Kaspar

Copyright © 2013 by Christopher J. Kaspar

All rights reserved.

No part of this book may be reproduced in any form or by any electronic or mechanical means including information storage and retrieval systems, without permission in writing from the author. The only exception is by a reviewer, who may quote short excerpts in a review.

Printed in the United States of America

First Printing: Dec 2013

ISBN 978-1483992556

10 9 8 7 6 5 4 3 2 1

Dedication

I dedicate this book to my three children, Jaslene, Cristian, and of course, Alexus, who give my life so much meaning.

As a parent, you always want what's best for your children and hope your vision and advice will lead them down the right path. Sometimes your vision can go off track and sometimes your advice can be forgotten.

As I wrote this book, I discovered there were three key elements that helped me accomplish my goal of writing this book.

1. A good support system to help you through thick and thin.

2. A clear vision of what you want to accomplish.

3. The desire to finish what you started.

My wish is for this book to act as a reminder for my children that they can accomplish anything they truly want in life.

With Love,

Dad

Contents

Chapter 1

An Introduction to First Impressions

*"We don't know where our first
impressions come from or precisely what
they mean, so we don't always appreciate
their fragility."*

Malcolm Gladwell

Imagine you work for a Fortune 500 company for a moment. As you evaluate yourself, you realize you're one of the best and brightest in your department. For some reason, less-talented and less-qualified people seem to be moving up the corporate ladder faster than you are. This is a common dilemma that many people find themselves in each year. You find yourself saying, "How in the world

> *For some reason, less-talented and less-qualified people seem to be moving up the corporate ladder faster than you are.*

did that person get that job in the first place?"

Now, let's switch gears for a second. Your boss calls you into her office and tells you to take a seat. She says, "I've been managing for over fifteen years. Your performance is one of the best I've ever seen." Then she says, "Do you think you have what it takes to get to the next level in the company?" This is the opportunity you've been dreaming about. What would you say? Then she says, "I want you to take my place at the executive holiday party next week. I know you won't know a soul at the party, but this is an excellent opportunity to network with senior executives, help get your name out there, and hopefully open new doors for you throughout the company." What would you be thinking?

"Your first impression in the business world is just as important as your talent."

Well, this is exactly where Ivan and Donna found themselves on a cold December day in Ms. Garrison's office. Donna moved her short dark hair out of her face and thought to herself, "I hate going to parties. I never know what to say." On the other hand, Ivan was delighted. He said, "Donna, we won't know anyone, but this is *a great* opportunity to meet new people, right?" Donna said, "Yeah, I guess so."

Ms. Garrison looked Donna directly in the eyes and said, "Your first impression in the business world is just as important as your talent." In this business your first impression can follow you for the rest of your career, so always try to make the best impression each and every time. It can make the difference between making the sale or losing the sale, or the difference between getting promoted or being passed over for a promotion."

Then Ms. Garrison said, "This is a great opportunity. Please take advantage of this opportunity tomorrow. I consider both of you to be the future of this company."

The next day Ivan and Donna drove to the holiday party. On the way there they agreed to split up so they could meet different people. Ivan was full of energy and was explaining to Donna that the CEO was going to be at this party. As they pulled up, Donna took a deep breath and said, "I can't wait for this party to be over." Ivan said, "Not me. There is no other place I'd rather be tonight. It's going to be exciting."

As they entered the ballroom, they could hear music in the background. The smell of hors d'oeuvres filled the room, and everyone seemed to be having a great time. Ivan quickly introduced himself to the first person he saw and started a conversation immediately. Donna started to walk around the ballroom, almost appearing lost. She felt uncomfortable, but said to herself, "If Ivan can do this, so can I." Donna noticed that a shorter woman with thin wire-frame glasses was standing by herself. She approached her and said, "Hello, my name is Donna." She said, "Hello, I'm Kim, nice to meet you." Donna then said, "Do you come to this party every year?" Kim replied, "No, it's my first time." Then Donna asked, "So, how's the food?" Kim responded, "It's okay."

Donna continued to ask different questions for the next two minutes, but Kim only replied to each question with a simple yes or no. Donna said, "It was nice meeting you" and moved on. She looked over in the corner and noticed Ivan laughing with two other people like they were old friends. Donna approached two other people but got the same results. No one answered her questions except with a yes or a no. After two minutes, she kept running out of things to say.

Donna was frustrated. She saw Ivan talk to at least a dozen people with ease. Donna said to herself, "How does Ivan do it?" Then a gentleman named Mike approached Donna. Mike started talking to Donna about the party, work, and the future of the company. He was very professional, but there was one problem. Mike just kept talking and talking. Donna didn't know how to stop the conversation. After forty minutes, Donna excused herself to the bathroom to get out of the conversation. As Donna and Ivan were leaving the party, people were actually saying good-bye to Ivan as though he were the CEO. On the drive home, Donna asked Ivan, "How were you able to do that tonight?" Ivan looked at Donna with a quizzical expression and said, "What do you mean?" Donna said, "I watched you connect with so many people at that party like they were your best friends. How were you able to make such a great first impression with total strangers?" Ivan looked at Donna with a puzzled face and said, "I don't know. Doesn't everyone do that at parties?" Donna said, "I just don't understand. I'm a good conversationalist with the people I know, but I go blank with strangers."

Over the next several weeks Donna started to observe Ivan much closer. She couldn't believe what she was seeing. Before the holiday party she viewed Ivan as an average Joe who liked to talk, maybe a little too much at times, but he wasn't better than her. He came in later than her, took longer lunch breaks, and was never as thorough in meetings or presentations. However, within every meeting with a new customer, Ivan was the superstar. He was the one customers wanted to talk to after the meeting. Ivan was the one they gave their business card to. Ivan was the one the customer always wanted to speak to on the phone. It didn't matter if the customer was male or female, younger or older, or even their race. She started to realize it wasn't just with new customers it was with anyone he came in contact with and every time she saw it she found herself

"I just don't understand. I'm a good conversationalist with the people I know, but I go blank with strangers."

saying the same thing "how does he always seem to make a great first impression with everyone?"

Fast forward 3 months. Donna got a real dose of reality, when for the first time in her career someone had better numbers for the quarter than she did. She almost fell out of her chair when she found out it was Ivan. The person she paid so little attention to and didn't think much of looked better than her on paper for the quarter.

How could this be? Donna was an A student, went to a better college, and worked harder than anyone in the department. Isn't that the formula for success in the business world?

Before we go any further in this book, let me ask you a few questions.

1. Who do you relate to better and why?

2. Why does Ivan always seem to appear like a superstar?

3. Why does Donna struggle?

4. Name at least one person you know similar to Ivan besides yourself. List three qualities that help them stand out among their peers

5. Name at least one person you know similar to Donna besides yourself. List three qualities that could help them stand out among their peers.

Regardless of what point you are at in your career it's critical to evaluate the people around you. You should always keep the mindset that you can always learn something new from anyone you meet and you always have something new to offer as well.

Fast forward six more months, Ms. Garrison just found out her assistant director Mr. Brawn decided to take a job outside the company. This put Ms. Garrison in a tough spot and she would need to fill the role immediately because she had several special projects in the pipeline. Hiring someone outside the company would take months and everyone within her team was critical. She talked to her bosses about possible candidates but kept coming up short. As she mapped out who could possibly take over the role she realized she had two up and coming superstars in the making and this would be a great experience for either of them and could possibly fast track their career. She only had one problem. She needed to ensure she was fair across the board for people applying for the job.

At her monthly meeting she broke the news to the team. She encouraged anyone interested to apply. Donna thought to herself immediately, "There's no way I would get that job." Ivan raised his hand and started asking questions like "What experience level are you looking for", "What skills do you need", and so on. At the end of Ivan's questioning Donna and Ivan decided to apply for the job.

Donna knew she was a poor interviewer. She studied a few books and read a dozen articles before the interview. As she walked into the interview and sat down at the table she realized across from her was a panel of five people including Ms. Garrison. Ms. Garrison opened the interview by asking, "Tell us a time you failed in your career and how you overcame it." Donna was stumped for a moment before saying, "I haven't experienced failure at this point in my career." Then Ms. Garrison said "If you haven't experienced failure than how will you deal with it once it's staring you directly in the eye and the clock is ticking?" Donna didn't have a good answer. She really struggled throughout the interview.

As for Ivan he prepared for the interview in a similar fashion as Donna looking for any new techniques he could use in the interview. Ms. Garrison opened the interview with the same question "Tell us a time you failed in your career and how you overcame it." Ivan had a different approach. He told a story about running out of gas his second day of work and explained how he ensures his car always has at least a quarter tank of gas Monday thru Friday. Then he told a story about him being in Boy Scouts and how his carelessness almost burned a thousand acres of land and now he carries the lesson of carelessness equals failure with him every day at work. Ivan was able to impress the panel from start to finish in the interview.

Ms. Garrison took all things into account and determined Ivan was the clear choice for the job. When Donna got the news she was very disappointed. She started thinking, maybe I was too young, not enough experience, it wasn't my time, but when she found out Ivan got the job she almost fell off a cliff. She asked Ms. Garrison to explain the differences between Ivan and herself. Ms. Garrison said "Donna interviews are tough and that is what this came down to. Ivan was a little better in the interview. Unfortunately, this is how the business world works. Your first impression in the business world via meetings, presentations, phone calls, social events, and even interviews can make or break a career."

Regrettably, Donna stayed in the same position for the next three years as she watched Ivan get promoted two more times.

Why This Book?

This book will take you on a journey to discover how to make a better first impression. You will also discover why it doesn't matter who you relate to better in the story. This book is intended to help you strengthen your skills so that you can connect with people better and faster as well as provide you with proven tools and techniques that can help you make a better first impression. Throughout the book, we will dissect Ivan and Donnas' night, looking for ways to improve it.

It is an unfair reality that your success in business largely depends on how people perceive you and on the relationships you create and keep. Another unfair reality is that so many of us spend most of our time focusing on the job itself, our career goals, and how to outperform our peers, never realizing we lack the skills it takes to create key business relationships on the fly which is considered the lifeline of business success for many people.

A common misconception is that you are either born with the gift of gab, or not. This book helps break those misconceptions and provides you with essential tools and techniques that you can instantly use to make a good first impression and build on that impression if you work on your skills. Good luck on your journey. Remember the skills you learn in this book can give you a competitive advantage in your career for years to come.

Chapter 2

Three Secrets to Excelling at Any Social Event

"I'm a firm believer in the theory that people only do their best at things they truly enjoy. It is difficult to excel at something you don't enjoy."

Jack Nicklaus

Throughout the book, we will refer back to Ivan and Donnas' journey. Let me ask you, why did Ivan do so well at the party? This is the million-dollar question for people who relate to Donna. It's easy to say that Ivan is a natural that he was born with the gift of connecting with people, or any number of reasons that people perceive how

they do it with ease. It is true that Ivan probably has some natural ability of connecting with others, but the truth is that Ivan isn't doing anything Donna can't do if she studies and applies the principles covered in this book. We have studied hundreds of people in the last few years to understand what commonalities people like Ivan share to make instant connections with others. We found three main commonalities that seem to be universal with people who always seem to make a great first impression with ease. The amazing thing we discovered is that people like Ivan rarely realize what they are doing.

Their energy and enthusiasm can lift people up, instantly putting others in a good mood ...

The first commonality that they share is a positive attitude. There are few things more pleasing when meeting a stranger than a positive attitude. People like Ivan tend to have a positive attitude no matter whom they are around. Their energy and enthusiasm can lift people up, instantly putting others in a good mood and leaving a memorable impression that this is a person I want to be around. If you recall in Chapter 1, as soon as Ivan got the news he was going to a party he said, "Donna we won't know anyone, but this is a *great* opportunity to meet new people, right?" Ivan took that positive attitude with him into the party. He used that energy with the first person he saw to help start a conversation with a stranger. It's amazing how far a positive attitude can take you in life, and it's even more amazing how many people don't utilize this attribute on a daily basis. John N. Mitchell, former Attorney General of the United States said it best "Our attitude towards life determines life's attitude towards us." We'll take a more in-depth look at this subject in the next chapter.

On the opposite side you may recall, Donna almost had the opposite attitude by saying to herself, "I hate going to parties." This type of attitude can become contagious. It can also be a deterrent as soon as you open your mouth. Scott Hamilton, an American Figure Skater and Olympic Gold Medalist once said "The only disability in life is a bad attitude." That's a very powerful statement considering millions of people deal with some sort of disability on a daily basis but still choose to look at life in a positive matter. What's your reason to wake up with a bad attitude? Remember the first secret. If you're going to make a good first impression, snap out of your mood and always look on the positive side of things.

The second commonality we found was preparation. What do I mean? Are people like Ivan studying other people and making notes so they have the perfect things to say all the time? The answer to this is an overwhelming "No!" From our observations, people like Ivan are either consciously or subconsciously prepared. When people are subconsciously prepared for conversation, they are so comfortable communicating with people that they have learned to organize their thoughts, ideas, and stories in a way that allows them to make connections easily. In many cases, they are also amazing storytellers with the ability to make a simple life-event interesting and funny. A good person to study that has made a career of this skill is Jay Leno. His unique combination of conversation skills, humor, and witty jokes make it hard not to like him almost immediately.

The ability to want to be somewhere drives your attitude, mood, and mindset before you even start.

This wasn't the case for Donna. She found herself in a number of dead-end conversations that lasted for only minutes. If you can relate to Donna, don't feel discouraged. This is a skill that can be learned with a little practice. Most comedians like Jay Leno and Jerry Seinfeld took years before they mastered their craft.

In the following chapters, you will find tools and techniques that will help you improve and master subconscious preparation for conversation. Remember, the second secret is preparation. It is also the foundation for a good conversation.

The final commonality is, wanting to be there. This is very imperative to understand. The ability to want to be somewhere drives your attitude, mood, and mindset before you even start. As Donna and Ivan got out of the car, the following conversation took place. Donna took a deep breath and said, "I can't wait for this party to be over." Ivan said, "Not me. There is no other place I'd rather be tonight. It's going to be exciting." As you can quickly see, Ivan genuinely wanted to be there while Donna couldn't wait to leave which killed her attitude before she stepped into the party. Has this ever happened to you? Did you have a good time and most importantly could you have had a better time it you wanted to be there?

In the following chapters you will discover tools and techniques to conquer this mindset. Remember, the final secret is, genuinely wanting to be there. This delivers that warm feeling a loved one gives us when you come home. It also drives a great attitude that instantly connects with others and creates a great first impression over and over again.

Activity:

1. List the three universal commonalities among those people who make a good first impression?

    1.

    2.

    3.

2. Which commonalities do you have?

3. Which commonalties do you need to work on?

Chapter 3

Why Do I Keep Failing at Social Events

"A failure establishes only this, that our determination to succeed was not strong enough."

~Hoshang N. Akhtar

Have you ever tried to start a conversation with a stranger and thirty seconds later you find

yourself out of questions and ready to never approach another person again? If you said yes, you are not alone. This has been the norm in my personal life for years. When I reflect on many of my conversations, I get even more frustrated because I knew I was a pretty good conversationalist with family and friends. Why would my mind go blank in these situations? Can you relate to my pain? Why do so many initial conversations go so bad?

As we focus on Donnas' night, we can quickly uncover a blueprint for failing to initiate conversations which is certainly a starting point for creating a bad first impression. There were two major factors that contributed to her failure.

Negative Self-Phrases

The first factor is what I call NSPs, or Negative Self-Phrases. NSPs are nothing more than common phrases we use to tell ourselves something negative will happen.

Here are some examples of NSPs:

- I can't do this.

- Those people will never like me.

- I shouldn't have come.

- I never do well at these things.

- I never have anything to say.

Do you remember the common phrase "believing is achieving"? Well, that phrase also works in a negative way. In Donna's case, she used two NSPs before she even walked into the event, therefore setting a foundation for failure. Donna's first NSP was "I hate going to parties". This set the mood for how she was going to approach the party.

Her second NSP was "I can't wait for the night to be over". NSPs are a very common cause of failure when we meet someone for the first time. The amazing thing is many times we don't even realize we're doing it.

Fear of failure contributes to a large portion of this mindset. If you believe you will fail, you will most likely look for reasons why things won't work out or talk yourself out of doing something before you start. A fear of failure is the biggest justification for this negative mindset. Think about it. We all like connecting with people (unless you're an engineer like me). If we knew we could make an instant connection with every person we met, I wouldn't be writing this book and social connections wouldn't be a problem for many people. However, since so many of us experience some level of fear during a conversation or have had an unforgettable experience that has led us to failure, we don't want to experience that feeling again. Therefore, if you are searching for reasons not to go to social events, not willing to approach new people, always trying to look busy with a cell phone, or counting down the seconds before you can leave, I have one question for you. How do you think you will make a good first impression if you have this negative mindset? Although you may be able to make a good first impression with a negative mindset, your chances are slim. Your negative energy will give off a negative vibe making you seem unapproachable or uninterested.

Positive Self-Phrases

There is only one way to prevent yourself from using NSPs. Instead of looking for reasons why you don't want to be there, start looking for reasons why you do want to be there. These reasons are known as PSPs, or Positive Self-Phrases. Remember every time you go somewhere, every time you meet someone new, it's an opportunity for you to grow.

Here are some examples of PSPs:

- I may meet someone of value.

- This is an opportunity to meet someone new.

- I may learn something new.

- I may be able to help this person, who might reciprocate later.

- This could open new doors.

If you really want to, you can turn any negative reasoning into positive reasoning.

NSPs are among the most common reasons why we fail to make a good first impression even before we start a conversation. This one factor can actually cancel out two of the three commonalities of why people excel. Those two commonalities are a positive attitude and wanting to be there. You are actually killing two birds with one stone and virtually ensuring failure before you even open your mouth when using NSPs.

The second most common factor of failure comes from a lack of preparation. This is why so many conversations with strangers last for thirty seconds or less. As mentioned in Chapter 2, a key commonality to make an instant connection is preparation. You must be consciously or subconsciously prepared. In Donna's case, she wasn't consciously or subconsciously prepared and was doomed before she opened her mouth. Donna actually had no idea how to keep the conversation going once she introduced herself.

The second most common factor of failure comes from a lack of preparation.

Here is an example of a type of conversation Donna had at the party:

Donna: "Hi, I'm Donna."

Alex: "Hi, my name is Alex."

Donna: "So, do you come to these conferences a lot?" (Donna was expecting a yes answer.)

Alex: "No."

Donna: "That's too bad. These conferences have great food." (Donna said this because she didn't know what else to say.)

Alex:	"Oh, that's good." (Donna lost the connection with Alex.)
Donna:	"So, do you like your job?" (Donna is trying to keep the connection going.)
Alex:	"It's okay, why do you ask?" (At this point, Alex is annoyed and he said this in a rude way.)
Donna:	"Just asking. Well, nice meeting you." (Donna is disengaged and ready to go.)

What did Donna do wrong? How could things have gone better? We will focus on how to better prepare for a conversation in the next chapter. It is vital to understand if you are going

Preparation is the lifeline for keeping a conversation going.

to make a good first impression, you need to be prepared. Preparation is the lifeline for keeping a conversation going. Some of us, like me, have to consciously prepare for a period of time before we are subconsciously ready. Utilizing the tools and techniques in the coming chapters gives you the necessary blueprint to ensure that you can keep almost any conversation going with ease. The key is to practice with these tools and techniques as much as possible so you can get to the point where you are subconsciously prepared for any conversation.

Activity:

Before I go any further with this lesson, here is an activity I do with my students. If possible, I have students partner up. Your partner is there to observe and take notes about your progress and to give you feedback. However, a partner isn't required.

Go into any safe social setting. It might be a party, mall, or an airport.

Seek to strike up a conversation with a total stranger. Try to have a genuine conversation with them. Your goal is to find out their mother's name without actually asking the question, "What is your mother's name".

Try to approach three people in a thirty-minute span. This can actually be harder than one may think, but once you start practicing it will become second nature.

Write notes about each conversation. Did you fail or succeed? Was the person open? What could you have done better? How did you get their mother's name?

Review:

Reasons why some people excel:

1. A positive attitude—There is no substitute for positive energy and enthusiasm. This type of energy will lift others instantly.

2. Preparation—Either consciously or subconsciously, other people always have plenty to talk about. Many people who excel in conversations usually are subconsciously prepared for conversation. This simply means these people are so comfortable having conversations with others they can easily organize their thoughts, ideas, and stories in a way that makes connections easily.

3. Wanting to be there—Focus on the positive side of why you're going to an event. Talking to new people will keep you in the right frame of mind.

4. Using Positive Self-Phrases—Telling yourself positive phrases to reinforce positive things will happen.

Reasons why other people fail:

1. Negative Self-Phrases (NSPs)—NSPs are nothing more than common phrases we use to tell ourselves that something negative will happen to us. The opposite of NSPs are PSPs or Positive Self-Phrases. This is simply

taking an NSP and looking at it from a positive perspective. For example:

- NSP–Why should I go when I won't know anyone?

- PSP–This is an excellent opportunity to meet new people.

2. Lack of preparation—Daily preparation is essential to making a good first impression. When a conversation goes down hill it can usually be contributed to not being prepared.

Chapter 4

It's the Preparation That Matters

"By failing to prepare, you are preparing to fail."

~Benjamin Franklin

Since there are numerous business settings for numerous types of business professionals, we will simply address them as events from now on. For example, if you are a salesman, the term "event" could really mean a sales meeting. If you are an engineer, the term "event" could be a technical exposition, or just a day at the office to you. Whatever your profession may be, feel free to substitute something relevant for the word "event."

At this point, you have

discovered that attitude, preparation, and the mindset of wanting to be there are the three major differences between people who excel and people who fail at making good first impressions in the business world. In the previous chapter, we focused on tools and techniques to help you with the attitude and mindset needed to be around other people. Before we move on to tools and techniques for preparation I want to reiterate the importance of your attitude. No matter where you are, you must always approach meeting new people and the prospect of new opportunities from a positive perspective. By doing this one simple thing, your chance of making a good first impression increases tenfold.

We are now at a good point to discuss being nervous. Being nervous can affect your attitude, mood, and train of thought. I used to get nervous pretty easily when I met strangers and I didn't understand how to handle it. My conversations were all over the place, and I always felt like an idiot. That is, I felt like an idiot until I had a conversation with Mr. Thomas.

As a young employee, I had the ambition of being an executive. Mr. Mike Thomas was the president of my business unit and is one of the best executive speakers I have ever heard. I wanted to be a presenter like him and to understand the secrets to his success. I decided to send him an e-mail letting him know I aspired to be a great presenter like him. To my delight, he replied to me and setup a one-on-one meeting for us. The day of our meeting, as I took the elevator to the seventh floor, my body was filled with nervous energy. I sat outside his office for about ten minutes before his receptionist called me in. I must admit I was a bit star struck when I entered his office. It was a corner office, similar to what a New York City executive in a movie would have. As we sat down on one of his leather sofas, I looked around and noticed almost a dozen awards spread around his office. For the next twenty-five minutes, he shared some of his amazing experiences with me as a presenter. But, it was his final point that taught me an invaluable lesson on dealing with nervous energy. I was getting ready to leave when Mr. Thomas realized that I had been nervous the entire time I was there. He said, "Look Chris, I know it must be intimidating to sit in this office and talk to the president of a Fortune 500 company, but I want you to understand something. I do business with some of the richest and smartest people in the world and that can be intimidating, but I remind myself of this small fact. I put my shirt on just like them, one arm at a time. I put my pants on just like them, one leg at a time, and it reminds me that we really aren't that different. "He continued, "Chris I put my shirt on just like you and I put my pants on just like you. The only real difference between you and me is that I run a two-billion dollar company and you don't." By the

I do business with some of the richest and smartest people in the world...

time I walked out of Mr. Thomas's office, I had learned an invaluable lesson. Regardless of whom you're talking to, they really aren't that much different from you. Realizing this point can calm your nerves before you start and make any conversation easier.

We will now focus on the essential tools and techniques you can use to prepare for conversations. Believe it or not, preparing for conversation is a skill that can be learned and fine-tuned. All of us have plenty to talk about. However, when it comes to strangers our minds can go blank. One of the easiest ways to find something to talk about on a daily basis is discovering a common interest. Believe it or not, keeping up with current events will always give you fresh material to talk about. I personally try to keep up with five major topics daily: current news, business, technology, sports, and entertainment. There are many other areas you can keep up with. Whatever interests you is fine. Keeping up with different current events will give you a vast resource of talking points in your mind to pull from on the fly. I generally spend about thirty to forty minutes on the Web researching this information. Here are the main Web sites I use:

> *Believe it or not, preparing for conversation is a skill that can be learned and fine-tuned.*

- www.cnn.com—Current News, Business, Technology, and Sports

- www.espn.com—Sports

- www.forbes.com—Business & Technology

- www.people.com—Entertainment

- www.aol.com—General stories

Your ability to know what's current and to discuss interesting articles can make you a hit virtually anywhere.

The second area that can give you leverage in a conversation are general topics such as books, hobbies, and common interests. One strategy I use in this department is talking about Malcolm Gladwell. He has published three phenomenal books:

1. *The Tipping Point*—This book describes how little things can make a big difference.

2. *Blink*—This book is about the power of thinking without thinking.

3. *Outliers*—This book tells the story of successes.

These books provide numerous fascinating conversational topics that most people can relate to. Reading them can help you create a fast connection.

Here are some sample discussion topics:

- How does a man with an IQ 30 percent higher than Einstein's IQ become a bouncer in New York City?

- Why can it be dangerous for doctors to have too much information?

- Why is the law of few so important to you?

- How do Asia kids really have a built in advantage in Mathematics?

All three of these questions can be answered in Malcolm Gladwell's books. Trust me, when I get into a conversation on those topics people want to keep talking.

If you spend at least 30 minutes a day driving to work every morning I highly recommend tuning into Hot 99.5 the Kane show in the Washington DC area. You can also download the smartphone app iHeartRadio if you don't live in the area. The Kane Show provides a daily lineup of entertaining stories and topics you can utilize at any time to integrate into your daily conversations.

The main radio personality, Kane, is an excellent storyteller with an uncanny ability to simplify even the most complicated stories on the fly. Kane creates almost instant rapport with his listener as a family man and by being very open about his personal life. Along with Kane and the other radio personalities on the show it provides a great mix of opinions that make the show a morning must.

A popular weekly segment of the show is called War of the Roses. Listeners submit stories about their partner possibility cheating and the radio personality Kane calls them offering free prizes, requesting information, etc... in order to get to the truth. Within a 5 minute time span Kane is able to build rapport, determine if they are cheating, and get the truth out of them.

Telling a personal story always keeps the conversation fresh and interesting...

One of my favorite episodes is when Kane talks a guy into believing he has a voice lie detector device that can determine stress patterns when he answers questions. Kane gets the truth about his cheating ways in about 5 minutes.

All War of the Roses segments are recorded as podcasts to listen to anytime. For more information please visit www.kaneshow.com.

The third area of preparing for conversation is telling stories. Telling an interesting story you read is fine, but keep in mind someone may have already read that story. Telling a personal story always keeps the conversation fresh and interesting if you know how to do it. Always, Always, ALWAYS stay away from stories that brag about yourself. It's okay to brag about other people, but not yourself. It can be a real turn-off when someone tells you how great she is. A great place to practice your storytelling is Toastmasters. Toastmasters International is a nonprofit worldwide organization focused on public speaking and leadership. You can find a club near you by going to www.toastmasters.org. This organization can help you with your storytelling as well as your public speaking skills. The cost is usually around $60 a year. It is a great investment in your future.

Telling stories is a skill. Some people are good at it and some aren't, but we can all improve on how we tell them. As you seek to improve your storytelling skills, first make a list of the following:

- Life lessons you have learned

  For example, my story about Mr. Thomas provided the lesson you're not that much different from others.

- Funny stories

- Famous people you have met

- Places you have visited

- College

- Your job

- And so on

As you create your list, you will find that you have some really cool stories you can tell. Next, write your stories out and figure out the point of each story. There is a simple phrase about storytelling that everyone should follow: tell a story and make a point. Many of us are bad storytellers because we tell stories that don't have a point.

After you write a story that has a point, practice telling that story at Toastmasters. One of the most important aspects of Toastmasters International is that they will provide instant feedback for your story. This feedback will help you fine-tune your stories. You can also watch other people tell stories and listen to their feedback. This can be invaluable and help you develop new ideas. This may seem like hard work, but trust me, people remember good stories.

Review:

A few tips on storytelling:

1. Make yourself human. People like to hear how you failed before you succeeded.

2. Practice bragging without bragging. The first time I met Dr. Wilson he said, "How did you win the Eagle award at the age of twenty-five?" In this example, someone else is asking about your accomplishment.

3. Make sure you have a point to your story.

Activity:

Make a list of at least 5 current events that you can talk about daily and list their sources. Put this on your daily to-do list.

1.

2.

3.

4.

5.

Make a list of five books that you can talk about with a broad audience. Make sure to only choose engaging stories from each book.

1.

2.

3.

4.

5.

Make a list of ten to twenty stories you can tell people. Practice these stories in front of friends and family. I strongly recommend you try them out at Toastmasters. Master the skill of storytelling and you will be a hit at any event.

Here are five topics to get you started:

1. Pets

2. Vacation

3. Childhood

4. Lessons taught to you by a hero

5. Lessons from work

6.

7.

8.

9.

10.

Chapter 5

Unlocking the Door to Good Communication

"Ah, good conversation - there's nothing like it, is there? The air of ideas is the only air worth breathing."

~ Edith Wharton

As you start a conversation and keep it going, it is essential to understand how to ask a question. If you recall, in Chapter 3 Donna had a conversation with Alex. No matter what Donna asked Alex the conversation turned into a dead-end. Donna found herself fumbling through multiple questions to attempt to create a conversation. Have you ever

found yourself in a situation similar to Donnas'? This can be a horrible experience for anyone. You find yourself asking ten to twenty questions in a row only to feel like you're invading the persons personal life and almost certainly making a bad first impression.

Well, I have the secret to ensure that never happens to you again. Before I give you the secret, you'll need to understand the two types of questions you can ask people:

1. Close-ended—These are the types of questions that can be answered with a simple yes, no, or short answer.

2. Open-ended—These are the types of questions that require an explanation.

If you haven't figured out the secret, it's open-ended questions.

Here are some examples of the words that most open-ended questions start with:

- How

- Why

- What

- Tell me

Asking these types of questions will start your conversation in the right direction every time and help you build on it.

Here are a few examples of open-ended questions I always use at events. I write them on the back of a business card just in case my mind goes blank.

- How are you connected to the event?

- What do you currently do? How did you get into that? What types of challenges do you have?

- If you weren't doing (fill in the blank), what do you think you would be doing?

- Where are you from? What was it like growing up there?

- What type of food do you like? Tell me about your favorite restaurant?

- How did you get interested in your career?

- For couples: How did you meet?

- Where do you live? How did you go about finding a place there?

- In what way do you think the country has changed?

- How did you ever wind up in that part of the world?

Using open-ended questions properly can immediately increase your likeability as you enter a conversation.

- What do you do when you're not working?

- What did you think of the performance?

- What do you recommend at the buffet?

Using open-ended questions properly can immediately increase your likeability as you enter a conversation. It can also increase your confidence, as we'll explore in later chapters.

As we finish this chapter, it is important to note that utilizing the tools and techniques in this book can differ between men and women.

Women must be aware and careful not to give the wrong signals to the opposite sex. This can be hard considering men can confuse almost anything for the wrong signal. If you are a woman in the business world, it is imperative to be conscious of men's reactions to you. If they misunderstand your kindness for something different or make you feel uncomfortable, please make your intentions clear immediately.

Men must be aware of overly aggressive behavior towards the opposite sex. It will create miscommunication and in the end will make you look bad. This is a business setting, so always look to keep it professional.

Activity:

1. What is a closed-ended question?

2. What is an open-ended question?

3. List 5 open-ended questions you can use at an event. Put them on the back of a business card and always carry it with you.

   1.

   2.

   3.

   4.

   5.

4. Why should you always act professionally and avoid creating mixed signals towards the opposite sex in business?

Chapter 6

Making Yourself Memorable in Fifteen Seconds or Less

"This is the last time you will ever see today, do something to make it memorable."

~ Anonymous

One of the most difficult aspects of making a good first impression is talking about yourself without  bragging. We have all met people who are full of themselves. What type of first impression did they leave on you? If you are the person who loves to talk about how great you are, stop now. One of the biggest turn-offs that prevents you from making a good first impression is appearing self-centered. For those who don't like to talk about themselves, the question becomes, how do I talk about myself so I don't appear self-centered?

As you try to make a good first impression, it is critical to know how to talk about yourself favorably without bragging. This is a critical skill that most people put very little effort into. I repeat, this is a critical skill and you can master it.

Over the next two chapters, we will explore the AHEAD technique. This technique is designed to help you instantly become more memorable, have people ask you to tell more about yourself, and allow you to easily connect with others.

In this chapter, we will focus on the first two elements of the AHEAD technique, which will help you develop a fifteen-second introduction about yourself. This is known as your elevator speech.

Before we go any further, let me give you a brief overview of the AHEAD technique. AHEAD stands for:

- **A**ttention Grabber

- **H**ave a benefit (to your target point, e.g., company or job)

---------- Fifteen-Second Elevator Speech ---------

- **E**ngage with a story

- **A**lways seek to make a connection

- **D**eliver a call to action

People who can clearly articulate what they do for a living appear more interesting and important almost instantly. In this chapter, you will discover how to make yourself instantly interesting and have other people give you permission to talk about yourself without bragging.

Utilizing the skills in this chapter will help you construct a fifteen-second elevator speech that will make others curious and cause them to ask you to talk more about yourself.

Attention Grabber

The opening sentence about you should stimulate curiosity and intrigue. When someone asks, "What do you do?"
What do you say? One of the most common mistakes people make in this department is giving a boring answer.  This is because they don't really put much thought into this aspect of themselves. Common answers include: "I'm a manager at X company," "I'm a real estate agent," or any other common reply that doesn't spark much interest.

Here are some examples of interesting openers:

- Real Estate Agent–"I help people find the keys to their dreams."

- Manager–"I help maximize talent to ensure business goals are met."

- Fashion Consultant–"I help people stand out in the crowd without saying a word."

You will immediately notice that none of these openers specify what the person's current job really is. Instead, each opener is a teaser that will grab the listener's attention.

Here are the three questions you need to answer to skillfully craft your opening sentence.

1. What do you do?

2. What are your responsibilities?

3. How do you help the company or target area?

Here are some sample answers:

1. What do you do? "I'm a Project Manager."

2. What are your responsibilities? "I manage and control cost, time, and customer requirements for multimillion-dollar customers."

3. How do you help the company or how do you solve problems? "I ensure the company meets customer expectations and improve project quality control,

identify, mitigate, and control risk management while maximizing company profits."

From that information, we can construct the following openers:

(Attempt 1) "I help manage project cost, time, and customer expectations to ensure my company reaches its maximum profit."

(Attempt 2) "I try to take multimillion-dollar concepts and turn them into profitable business ventures."

Attempt 1 is a good start but attempt 2 hits all the marks for creating that "Tell me more factor".

Remember:

1.   Clarity is essential for creating a successful elevator speech. Ask yourself: Can a sixth grader understand this?

2.   Think big, think out of the box, and remember your job is important.

3.   Come across as personable, not rehearsed. You don't need to be perfect.

Note: It is vital to understand your audience. If you're talking to people within your field or industry, you may want to have a second opener in your back pocket that gets a little more specific. The above openers are designed to spark interest in someone who isn't familiar with your field or industry.

You may have noticed I added a little humor in attempt two by adding the word "try." If you can add humor into your opener, it will most likely score you some extra points as you seek to make a good first impression.

If you can add humor into your opener, it will most likely score you some extra points...

Have a benefit

After you form your attention grabber, you will need to have a benefit associated with your opener. This will tell people why you have a cool job.

Before we go any further, it's critical to understand the difference between benefits and features. This always creates confusion in my classes.

Here are a few ways to remember the difference between features and benefits.

If you're talking about a car:

A feature of the car is the *air conditioning.*

A benefit of the car is the *comfort* you will receive from the air conditioner in the summer.

Remember: A feature belongs to the product or service.

A benefit is the experience or what you gain from the product or service.

Write down five benefits that relate to what you do.

1.

2.

3.

4.

5.

Flash back to the project manager's opener:
I try to take multimillion-dollar concepts and turn them into profitable business ventures.

Now we need to find a benefit associated with this job. Here are some phrases you may wish to use:

1. I help bring customer ideas to life.

2. My job allows me to continuously use my problem-solving skills.

3. I enhance customer satisfaction.

4. I'm able to travel and see the world.

5. My job allows me to meet a lot of interesting people.

Benefits statement

Being a project manager is great because it allows me to help my customers bring their ideas to life as well as utilize my problem-solving skills to enhance customer satisfaction.

We just formed a fifteen-second elevator speech. Now there are two ways you can utilize your elevator speech.

1.   You can open with your attention grabber and wait for someone to ask you to explain further. A sample conversation with a contact you meet at an event could go as follows:

Contact: "So what do you do?"

You: "I try to take multimillion-dollar concepts and turn them into profitable business ventures."

Contact: "Oh, really? What does that entail?"

You: "Well, being a project manager is great because it allows me to help my customers bring their ideas to life as well as utilize my problem-solving skills to enhance customer satisfaction."

2.   You can also open by combining your attention grabber and benefit.

Contact: "So what do you do?"

You: "Great question. I try to take multimillion-dollar concepts and turn them into profitable business ventures. It's great being a project manager because it allows me to help my customers bring their ideas to life as well as utilize my problem-solving skills to enhance customer satisfaction."

It is up to you which elevator speech you want to use, but remember that you're having a conversation you're not making a presentation or trying to sell something.

Activity:

1. List three Attention Grabbers you can use

    1.

    2.

    3.

2. List three Benefit Statements you can use

    1.

    2.

    3.

Chapter 7

Getting Ahead in Any Conversation

"The secret of getting ahead is getting started."

~Mark Twain

Since you were introduced to the AHEAD technique in the last chapter, you learned how to create your elevator speech. In this chapter, I will help you bring the AHEAD technique full circle. For many years, I struggled in my own life to strike up a conversation, so I created the AHEAD technique through trial and error. The AHEAD technique acts as a framework to help you become more interesting and more memorable when starting a conversation and increases your chances of making a good first impression.

Let's quickly review the AHEAD technique:

- **A**ttention grabber
- **H**ave a benefit

- **E**ngage with a story

- **A**lways seek to make a connection

- **D**eliver a call to action

Engage with a story

Let's dive into the third part of this technique—engage with a story. This is where you seek to tie an interesting story to your elevator speech. This story should last two to three minutes, in most cases. The story will give people a better understanding of your elevator speech.

Here are a few examples of how you can transition into this. Start your transitions with these phrases:

1. Are you familiar with…?

2. Have you heard about…?

Engaging with a story can really increase your credibility as you talk about what you do. Again, I emphasize that you should stay away from bragging about yourself and focus on your job and other people who have helped you within your stories.

Here is an example of how to tie in the first three parts, A-H-E.

Contact: "So what do you do?"

You: "I try to take multimillion-dollar concepts and turn them into profitable business ventures."

Contact:	"Oh, really? What does that entail?"
You:	"Well, being a project manager is great because it allows me to help bring life to customer ideas as well as utilize my problem-solving skills to enhance customer satisfaction."

Here is where you can engage the other person's interest with a story such as the following:

"For example, imagine a client wants to build the tallest building in the world or build a  new product. Where do you start? How do you figure out how much it would cost? How long would it take? A company would hire me to understand their vision and it's my job to bridge that vision into an affordable solution."

At this point, I've created a pretty good picture of what I do. Hopefully, it will create some interesting conversation exchanges. This is exactly what the technique should do for you.

Always seek to make a connection

As we move into the fourth part of the technique—Always seek to make a connection—you'll need to remember you're throwing the ball back into your listener's court. You now need to check in with the other person. Immediately after your story, ask him an open-ended question that puts the focus back

Remember always try to make a connection by focusing on their likes, not yours.

on him. You are looking for connection points or conversation points with their real interest to build on. It is very important to note when you're building on a conversation you should always have back-to-back open-ended questions at your disposal. This simply means when you ask an open-ended question you also have a follow up open-ended question to build on to keep things flowing with ease. For example you may ask "How are you connected to the event", then based on their response you may follow it up by saying something like "That's interesting, how did you get involved with…". It can be easy to ask that first open-ended question and then forget to follow it up with a second open-ended question to keep things going with ease.

A good lead in is to ask about their profession and how they choose that field. You also may have already discovered a conversation point before you entered into the AHEAD technique. If this is the case, try to go back to that connection point and build on it. For example, if you discovered in the beginning of your conversation that the person is from Washington, DC, and likes the Redskins (Washington, DC's professional football team), you can now talk about the players and the upcoming season if you keep up with that team. Try to stay away from talking about how much you love your football team unless they give you permission in the conversation. Remember always try to make a connection by focusing on their likes, not yours. This will help you reestablish a connection and build on it. Also, try to decide whether you want to continue the conversation or not. Remember, you're never going to please everyone, so don't worry about it.

Another tool to keep in your back pocket when you're at this point in the conversation is building on the most persuasive word in the English language. Yale University did a study on the 12 most persuasive words and discovered the word "you" is the most persuasive word in the English language. Staying away from the word "I" and focusing on the word "you" in your conversations will make you appear more interested and more interesting in every conversation.

As you find connection points or areas of common interest, look to discover if you or someone else you know can help their cause.

For instance, if they spend time with a charity, maybe you can help or know someone who might help their charity. This will help increase your chances of making a connection, building your network, and making a good first impression. After you make a connection with an area of common interest, it's time to move into the last step of the AHEAD technique.

Deliver a call to action

As we move into the final step of the AHEAD technique—deliver a call to action—you're really seeking to connect with her after the conversation. At this point, you may think to yourself, "How do I get out of a bad conversation?" We will explore that in Chapter 13, How to Terminate a Conversation. Delivering a call to action is nothing more than giving the action to follow up at a later date.

Here are a few ways to deliver a call to action:

> You: "Do you have a business card? I think I may know a few people who could help you."

> You: "How does your calendar look next month? I'd love to discuss that further."

The AHEAD technique is a powerful tool. It does take some work to put together and you will need to practice it continuously. However, when you master this tool, you will increase your chances of building on a good first impression by tenfold. I recommend practicing your material with family, friends, and co-workers every chance you get.

Activity:

1. Write down five possible stories you could use with your elevator speech.

2. Try these stories with friends and family to determine which stories are the most engaging.

3. Practice transitioning from your story back to the other persons interests with an open-ended question.

Review:

The AHEAD technique

- **A**ttention grabber—Create an opening statement that will stimulate curiosity and cause intrigue about yourself.

- **H**ave a benefit (to your target point, e.g., company or job)—Share an interesting experience you gained from your job.

- **E**ngage with a story—Entice with an interesting story.

- **A**lways seek to make a connection—Put the focus back on him and try to connect with him.

- **D**eliver a call to action—Seek to connect with him at a later date.

Chapter 8

The Key to Making a Good First Impression

"What I am after is the first impression."

~Pierre Bonnard

At this point in the book we have really focused on two of the three elements that make up a good first impression:

- Attitude

- Preparation

Now it's time to put it all together. The final element of making a good first impression is building rapport. Building rapport is nothing more than creating a mutual feeling of trust. I think most of us have experienced this. Do you recall meeting someone for the first time and instantly feeling like the best

> *Building rapport is nothing more than creating a mutual feeling of trust.*

of friends? That feeling was instant rapport, and 99 percent of the time we have no idea why it happens.

As we try to build instant rapport, it's critical to understand the most important aspect of communication is the receiver. I think it's essential to reiterate this point. The most important aspect of communication is the receiver. This means building rapport is not about what we say as much as how others receive it. This is why building rapport can be so difficult.

Reducing Negative Snap Judgments

When building rapport, you must first try to reduce negative snap judgments. It is also a fact that attractive people have an advantage over others during initial contact. It is a fact that taller men have an advantage over shorter men during initial contact. As most people can't control these attributes about themselves it's imperative when you meet someone, look to reduce your snap judgments and give them a chance.

The second aspect of reducing negative snap judgments deals with how others perceive you.

The second aspect of reducing negative snap judgments deals with how others perceive you. Before I go any further, I want to make a point that these rules are unfair, but unfortunately, a lot of the world is based on snap judgments.

As you look at reducing the impact of snap judgments, let's first focus on your appearance.

The three aspects of appearance are health, grooming, and wardrobe.

I'm not an expert in these areas and advise you to talk to a consultant.

1. **Health**

   A. Maintaining your health is essential, not only for your appearance, but for yourself. If you want to lose a few pounds, I recommend you speak to a certified nutritionist. A nutritionist can put you on a diet plan that best works for you.

   B. Working out allows you to stay in shape and feel good. I recommend that you speak to a professional trainer to help find a workout program that best works for you.

   C. Finally, you need to ensure that you get a good night's sleep. Eight hours is recommended.

2. **Grooming**

   There are a number of things we can do to ensure good grooming. Here are some checklists:

Women

A.   Have neatly manicured nails.

B.   Maintain white teeth and fresh breath.

C.   Wear neutral makeup.

D.   Wear a touch of perfume.

E.   Have an up-to-date hairstyle.

Men

A.   Have neatly trimmed nails.

B.   Maintain white teeth and fresh breath.

C.   Have clean-cut or neatly-trimmed facial hair.

D.   Wear a touch of cologne.

E.   Have a nice haircut.

3.   **Wardrobe**

One of the biggest problems with wardrobes is that so many people tend to pick clothes based on what they like and not on what fits right.

My first recommendation is to go see a tailor. A tailor will take accurate measurements to ensure your clothes fit properly. If you have gained or lost more than ten pounds, you probably want to get your clothes tailored or get new clothes.

My second recommendation is to make sure your wardrobe compliments your skin tone. This simply means certain colors may look better on you than others do. I recommend talking to a fashion

Once you have maximized your appearance, you'll need to minimize your bad habits. It is normal when meeting someone for the first time to have nervous energy. However, this nervous energy usually leads to some bad habits. Bad habits that we aren't aware of can lead to negative snap judgments. We must first be aware of them before we can control them.

Make sure your wardrobe compliments your skin tone.

Some examples of bad habits are:

- Speaking in a monotone voice
- Fidgeting with your head, face, or lips
- Playing with things in your hands
- Moving around in your seat

SOFTEN

To minimize your bad habits, I recommend utilizing the SOFTEN technique. I came across this technique from Don Gabor. I have a slightly different version of SOFTEN, but still want to give Don credit for this technique. Here is my version:

Smile—Remember to smile once a minute.
Open posture—Stand with confidence and allow your body to be open and inviting.
Forward lean—Lean forward to show interest in the conversation.
Tone of voice—Speak in a calm and unhurried tone of voice.
Eye contact—Try to make eye contact 70 to 80 percent of the time.
Nod head–Nodding your head shows that you're interested in the conversation.

Utilizing the SOFTEN technique will make you appear more confident and positive as soon as you start a conversation.

Mirroring Body Language

Mirroring

Once you reduce negative snap judgments, it's time to synchronize yourself with the other person. This technique is called mirroring. Essentially, what you're doing is mirroring the other person's body language, facial expressions, vocal tone, rate, pitch, and gestures to some degree. You must do this in a subtle way so the other person doesn't notice you mimicking them. As you look at the picture on the previous page, you will see an image of what mirroring looks like. You can see that their legs are in the same position, their hands are in the same position, and their bodies are pretty much in the same position. Using this mirroring technique along with a good attitude and finding common ground in your conversations will allow you to synchronize yourself with the other person. At this point, you are creating rapport. As you stay in this zone, the other person will start to mimic your movements subconsciously. Staying in this zone helps you create a mutual feeling of trust and both of you will get the feeling of "I just met you, but I feel like we could be best friends."

Women tend to be more in tune with their emotions than men.

Kevin Hogan makes the point that mirroring the opposite sex can be a challenge for a number of reasons.

Men mirroring women

Women tend to be more in tune with their emotions than men. This is a common drawback to conversations because many men mask their feelings and show very little emotion in their faces. Mirroring a woman's facial expression is key when building rapport with her. When mirroring a woman's expression a man appears more interested, more interesting, more intelligent, and more attractive. This is why looks don't always matter to a woman. Hint, hint.

Women mirroring men

Men tend to use their bodies a lot more than their emotions. Therefore, when women try to mirror a man they shouldn't focus all their attention on the emotional state of their face or what they are feeling. Instead, try to use less facial expressions and mirror his body language. Businesswomen who maintain a serious expression are described by men as more intelligent, sensible, and astute.

Always Remember Names

When you are in synch with another person, it is significant to always remember names. Have you ever met someone and five seconds later you've already forgotten his name? It can be an embarrassing feeling and most people go through this dilemma their entire lives. The most common reasons given for this problem are:

- They are bad with names
- They have a bad memory

- And so on

The fact is these are excuses. The main reason we forget names so quickly is because we weren't listening in the first place. Often, we were already thinking about something else and never really heard them say their name. As soon as you're introduced to a person say, "Nice to meet you." Then, say their name. Do this even when you meet a group of people. This technique forces you to take a second and really hear the person's name. Yet, your work has only started. There are plenty of techniques out there to help you remember names. I'll share two of the most effective techniques that I use.

> *The main reason we forget names so quickly is because we weren't listening in the first place.*

1. **Name Association**

   When someone tells me their name I associate it with someone I know or someone famous. For example, if I meet a Bob I say to myself Bob, Bob, *Bob the Builder* (from the children's television show). I once met a guy named Marlin, which isn't a common name where I'm from. I called him Florida Marlin to myself and he was actually impressed I remembered his name the following week.

2.   **Repetition**

This is repeating a name over and over again in your head, then using their name in as many sentences as you can. For example, instead of saying, "So, how are you connected to the party?" Say, "Bob, how are you connected to the party?"

> *A conversation can turn negative in a flash depending on the other person's comments.*

Remain Positive

Another technique that will help you stay consistent is remaining positive. A conversation can turn negative in a flash depending on the other person's comments. No matter what, always appear positive. You do this for two reasons:

1.   If you're negative, it can make you look bad and you lose rapport instantly.

2.   If the other person is negative and you agree with him, he could go back and tell people you agreed, making you look

even worse. If this happens you can use Chapter 11, which will give you some ideas on how to save face and give neutral comments.

Time Active Listening

Once you reduce negative snap judgments and build rapport, you must keep it going. This is done through active listening. As you ask open-ended questions you must actively listen for key wants and needs. You can keep building on these within the conversation.

Here are some examples:

If we go back to page 10, you'll remember Donna was struggling to start a conversation with Kim. Donna asked Kim, "Do you come to this party every year?" Kim said, "No, it's my first time." Donna could have actually built on that conversation by saying. "This is my first time too. My boss actually gave me tickets. How did you get tickets to this event?"
Another example:

Today you decide to ride the metro. At your first stop an older women decides to sit next to you.

You start by saying "Hello" and smiling. (You're looking for a "Hello" and a smile in return).

Then you say, "I don't usually ride the metro, but today is a great day. So, what brings you to the metro today?"

She says, "Well, I usually take it to go to work, but today I'm going to meet my grandson from New York."

From that exchange there are three major topics you can build on. Here are some questions you can ask in each topic:

While you ask open-ended questions, you must actively listen for key wants and needs to build on.

Work

- Where do you work?

- How did you get involved in that field?

Grandson

- What are your plans with your grandson today?

- What's the most interesting experience you've had with him?

Family from New York

- How did your family end up in New York?

- What's been your favorite experience in New York?

While you ask open-ended questions, you must actively listen for key wants and needs to build on. As you build on what is being said, you must time your active listening so you can smoothly transition from one topic to another, focusing on the other person. The reason why this may seem hard is that many times we want to squeeze things in about ourselves. Remember, no one cares about you. They care about themselves. The key take away here is to focus on the

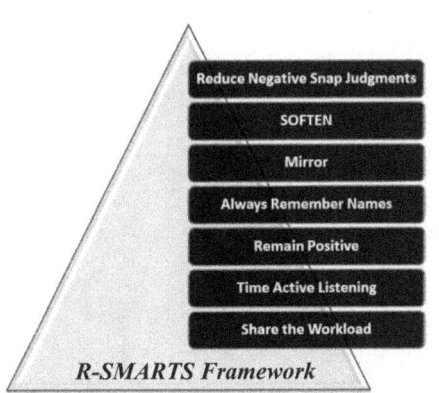

R-SMARTS Framework

other person and on what is being said. Then time your active-listening skills to easily transition from topic to topic and build on it.

Share the Workload

Sharing the workload is nothing more than reciprocating actions. For instance, I open the door for you so you may open the door for me. What you're really trying to do here is watch for the things you did to be returned. This includes offering actions or items of similar value, trying to help their cause, getting them connected to other people, etc. This really ensures that you will keep and grow the relationship after the first impression.

Review:

R-SMARTS is a seven step process for building rapport

1. Reduce negative snap judgments and reduce how others perceive you negatively.

    List 3 aspects of negative snap judgments

    1.

    2.

    3.

2. SOFTEN them up—Minimize your bad habits.

    List the elements that make up the SOFTEN technique

    S

    O

    F

    T

    E

    N

3. Mirror their movement—Synchronize yourself with the other person.

    What are the differences between mirroring men and women?

4. Always remember names—Pay attention when someone tells you their name.

   Why do people forget names so quickly?

   List two techniques to remember names?

   1.

   2.

5. Remain positive—Always appear positive.

   List two reasons why you want to stay away from being negative.

   1.

   2.

6. Time active listening—Actively listen for key wants and needs.

   Why is it important to utilize this skill?

7. Share the workload—Reciprocate actions.

   Why is it important to utilize this skill?

Chapter 9

The Secret Formula to Putting It All Together

"The thought that comes out is, maybe there's a good reason it's a secret."

~Ben Rudolph

As you recall, the critical elements needed to make a good first impression are:

- Attitude

- Preparation

- Rapport

You're now ready to put it all together. When putting it all together the first question you need to ask yourself is, "How do I open a conversation?" If you can remember this question,

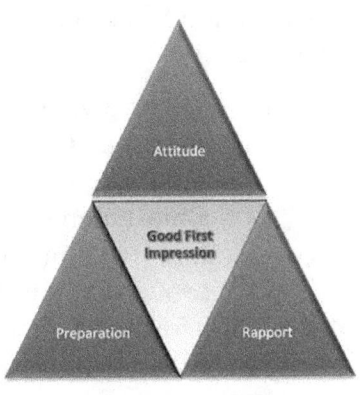

$A + P + R = GFI$

you will remember the secret formula called "The OPEN formula".

The OPEN formula is a framework for making a good first impression from start to finish. Here it is:

When you are trying to initiate a conversation, it is important to observe your environment.

- **O**bserve your environment.

- **P**osition to listen.

- **E**xplore for more.

- **N**ever neglect yourself.

Observe Your Environment

When you are trying to initiate a conversation, it is important to observe your environment. Observing your environment is also the first part of the OPEN formula. This is the key to starting the conversation. You can quickly do this in two ways:

1. Observe your environment and make a comment. Of course, the comment should be something positive. It is almost human nature and much easier to find something wrong, but starting a conversation in a negative way reflects poorly on you and increases your chances for a negative snap judgment.

When following these steps it's okay to throw out test questions to get a feel for the person. Here is an example:

You: "How are you doing?" Remember to smile. Observe the response. Some people just don't want to be bothered or their mind may be somewhere else at the time. Whenever this is the case don't take things personally. If you get a mediocre response, you can still make a comment. A sample conversation might be:

You: "That book looks familiar, what's the title?"

Contact: "The title is XYZ. Have you read it?"

You: "No, I've never read that book, but it looks interesting. Can you tell me what it's about?"

2. The second way is giving a compliment. Observe the person you want to talk to and find something they are wearing that you can identify and give a compliment on.

Here are some examples of what you can talk about:

A.   Shoes (always a safe bet)

B.   A woman's accessories

When the contact responds, you can reply with an open-ended question. By bringing a good attitude and practicing the first part of the formula, you will find out how easy it is to start a conversation. As soon as you initiate a conversation, start utilizing your R-SMARTS to build rapport. As you initiate the conversation you want to appear confident and positive so you can utilize the SOFTEN technique.

When building on a conversation and making the connection it can be easy to...

Position to Listen

When building on a conversation and making the connection it can be easy to get caught up in the conversation and forget to introduce yourself or exchange names. If you haven't gotten a name within the first five minutes, offer your name and your hand. This will almost always force the other person to shake your hand and give you their name. Try to match the pressure of the other person's handshake and remember their name, either by name association or name repetition.

As you remember their name, remember to always remain positive. I seem to repeat this point a lot, but I can't repeat it enough. It's also critical to remember that the other person may be nervous. They may start talking in a negative way. Remain optimistic and positive in your conversation. In Chapter 11, you will learn how to deal with negative undertones in a neutral way. Try to always talk in terms of the other person's interest and listen for more to talk about.

Explore for More Information

Exploring for more information means that you take key information you heard earlier and build on it to keep the conversation going. That's why it's imperative to understand and utilize the "time-active listening" tool you learned in the R-SMARTS technique. You can utilize that information in three ways:

1. **Fact disclosure**

   This is where you can talk about yourself in order for her to talk about herself. For example, you may say, "Yes, I attended Duke University for four years. Where did you go to school and what interested you in your major?"

2. **Sharing viewpoints and opinions**

   Be careful about sharing opinions on controversial topics. Sports, award shows, and anything else the other person can't take offense to are good choices. This helps maintain the personal connection.

3. **Express personal feelings**

This must be done with skill, but if you're in a conversation at this level, it's okay. For example, you might say, "Yes, I remember when my son was born like it was yesterday. It was…"

The deeper you connect the better your chances are of building rapport. Try to utilize the last part of the R-SMARTS technique and share the workload as you try reciprocating actions with them.

Never Neglect Yourself

Utilize the second part of the AHEAD technique **E-A-D** for the best results.

- You can talk about yourself.

- You can build on the conversation a little more.

- You can close the conversation.

By utilizing the OPEN formula, you can seamlessly increase your chances of connecting with other people, though it's noteworthy to understand that you will never connect with everyone you meet. It is human nature to worry about the people who you don't connect with, but many times it's not you, it's them. If that happens, don't worry about it. Move on. Try to focus on the people who want to engage with you and you will be fine with this secret formula. Focus on people worth your time and not on the people who aren't worth your time.

> *It is human nature to worry about the people who you don't connect with....*

Review:

As you utilize the OPEN formula, remember that the SOFTEN, R-SMARTS, and AHEAD techniques are also being used. Here is a review:

Observe your environment

    1.   Reduce negative snap judgments.

    2.   SOFTEN them up.

    3.   Mirror their movement.

Position to listen

    1.   Always remember names.

    2.   Remain positive.

Explore for more topics

    1.   Time active listening.

    2.   Share the workload.

Never neglect yourself

    1.   Use the AHEAD technique.

Chapter 10

Creating a Conversation without Saying a Word

"To say nothing, especially when speaking, is half the art of diplomacy."

~Will Durant

The next time you go to an event, a mall, or any other outing, take a few minutes to just sit and observe your environment. From time to time, you will witness people coming up to another person and starting a conversation. Ninety-nine percent of the time, the person they are speaking to isn't famous, nor do they have any special ability. They are usually your ordinary person next door.

So, what is their magic ability? Why are strangers walking up to them and starting conversations with them effortlessly? Often, the secret

will lie in their attire or accessories. Can you believe that's the secret? You're not impressed, I see. Well, if you utilize this correctly you can start instantly building rapport without saying a word because you have something that relates to them. This is a powerful tool you can use over and over again.

Let me give you an example:

Let's say that you want to make a good first impression with a new boss or a client. You ask around and find out that the person likes your favorite team. (Let's say it's the Pittsburgh Steelers).

When using this technique you may do the following:

Male—Wear a pin or a tie with the Steelers logo with your suit.

Women—Wear a necklace or earrings with the Steelers logo.

There are two situations where you can use this to your advantage:

1. You can hope the person who you want to start the conversation with sees what you're wearing.

2. You can utilize the OPEN formula with the other person and chances are they will notice your accessories and it will help you build rapport.

Your accessories may create a number of conversations on a given outing. It is essential to keep in mind you never know who you're talking to, so always treat everyone with respect and never underestimate this tool.

Now let's focus on accessories you can use that can help you create a conversation without saying a word.

Shirts are a great tool for everyone. Here are some examples of graphics on shirts that can start a conversation:

1. Sports

2. Funny movies

3. Funny sayings

Although shirts can be a great way to start a conversation, there are a few topics to be careful with. Here are a few examples of those types of graphics:

If someone has a very strong viewpoint on the opposite side of an issue, the conversation can quickly become negative.

1. Politics

2. Religion

3. Negative references

Consider that everyone isn't going to share your viewpoints. If someone has a very strong viewpoint on the opposite side of an issue, the conversation can quickly become negative. This can create a bad first impression without you even saying a word.

Other Accessories and Attire Men Can Utilize

Ties—Get ties that stand out. Ties with the following themes work well:

1. Disney

2. Sports

3. Movies

These ties may seem silly or like something you may never wear, but they are exactly what will make you stand out at any event and can bring enough attention to you that conversations will come to you.

Pins—Pins are a little harder to see and probably should only be worn with a suit, but they are great conversation magnets. You can wear pins from associations you support, your company, your sports team, or even from places you have visited. The key thing to understand here is pick one and stick with it.

Necklace Charms—There are thousands of charms you can choose from. Choose wisely and utilize them as positive conversation starters. Many people wear charms based on their religious preference. There is nothing wrong with this and I don't want to discourage anyone, but always be aware that some ignorant people can make negative snap judgments against you. It's your job to reduce as many of these negative snap judgments as possible.

Rings—High school, college, championship, or any other custom ring can bring you conversation.

Other accessories and attire you can use for drawing conversation to you include:

- For your head, face, and neck—stylish glasses, hats, scarves, and tie clips

- For your upper body—cufflinks, suspenders, stylish watches, bracelets, and other jewelry

- For your lower body—belts, shoes, and socks

Accessories and Attire for Women

Hairstyle, hair clips, and hair ties—Have a current hairstyle. If you color your hair, choose a color that flatters you and your style. Unique hair clips and ties can draw positive attention from others to help start a conversation.

Hats, scarves, and belts—When using these accessories, use them as stand-out pieces to accentuate your outfit, not to overwhelm it. If overdone, these accessories can turn into a negative snap judgment, keeping people away instead of inviting them in.

Earrings, necklaces, bracelets, watches, and other jewelry—Again, with these pieces the more unique or stylish they are, the more attention they catch.

Shoes and handbags—Women love their shoes and handbags. A great pair of shoes or a great handbag is sure to grab the attention of many women. They will also start great conversations since many women like to share their insights on their favorite shoes and handbags as well as their favorite designers.

A great pair of shoes or a great handbag is sure to grab the attention of many women.

Nails—You always want to make sure you have nicely manicured fingernails and toenails. Manicured nails help your jewelry stand out. You don't want anyone checking out a great piece of jewelry, only to be turned off by badly kept nails. Poorly groomed nails will turn the conversation from positive to negative because the other person may subconsciously make a negative snap judgment about you. The same applies to your toenails. A great pair of shoes deserves a great pedicure.

Even though I've provided a list of accessories and attire that may generate conversation, by no means am I a professional in this area. I recommend talking to a fashion consultant to help you put something together that works for you.

Activity:

Make a list of accessories you currently have that could draw a conversation to you.

1.

2.

3.

4.

5.

Make a list of accessories you might want to invest in.

1.

2.

3.

4.

5.

Chapter 11

The Dos and Don'ts of First Impressions

"A life spent making mistakes is not only more honorable but more useful than a life spent doing nothing."

~George Bernard Shaw

In this chapter, we will focus on some common dos and don'ts of initial conversations that can help you as you prepare to make a good first impression. One of the first questions I'm always asked is, "How should I approach strangers". This depends. In a business environment, utilize the OPEN formula. If you're in a social setting, you can do this in a few different ways.

> *One of the first questions I'm always asked is, "How should I approach strangers".*

1.   Keep in mind, it's always easier to approach someone who is alone. If you are at an event and you want to start a conversation, look for someone who is alone, and then use the OPEN formula. Chances are that person will be relieved you have started a conversation.

2.   If you don't see anyone alone, look for groups of three or more. Observe the group and identify the person doing the least amount of talking. When the time is right, approach that person and use the OPEN formula.

When done correctly, you can make a connection quickly and make an outstanding first impression with ease.

Another technique to add to your tool belt is the "fade into". This method requires you to wait in the background and listen to a conversation. When you hear something you can comment on and recognize that your comment will add value to the conversation, go ahead and comment, fading into the conversation. If done  correctly, the others in the conversation won't even know what you've done.

Never approach a group that looks engaged in an intense conversation. You are the outsider, and you will remain one. There is too much risk involved in attempting to join in. Another area you want to avoid is pairs or couples. Again, there is too much risk in approaching them, and you may be invading their space.

Before the event arrive early

It's essential to be familiar with your environment. If you're going somewhere new, it's imperative you get there early, check out the setting, know where the bathrooms are, and identify other logistical facts. These are important because you can use them to your advantage as you start a conversation. Arriving early also allows you to map out the place. You can choose the best seating, and you can get an idea of where the most traffic will be. This can be critical if you want to meet someone for the first time at an event.

Know whom you want to meet

If you're going to an event and you know who is going to be there, it may be to your benefit to choose a couple of people from the guest list whom you know you want to meet. It is your preference who it could be, but make sure you have something to offer in the conversation. It may be easy to pick out the most important person in the room, but remember that person will have many people approaching them. What do you have to offer that others don't? How will he or she remember you? Remember, choose wisely.

Minimize your drinks

This is easy to say but more significant to do. Some of us may have a drink or two, but remember the more you drink the more vulnerable you become. My rule of thumb is never drink in front of people you don't know.

Don't prejudge

Just as we hope others are not prejudging us, it's critical for us to eliminate our own snap judgment of others. Strive to have an open mind, and give everyone the same chance.

Don't sit with people you know

It is an automatic habit to look for people we know and sit with them. However, this doesn't expand your contact base. Take into consideration, sitting with new people forces you to practice your new skills.

Make eye contact

Try to stay focused on the other person. It can be easy to get distracted with other thoughts, your own responses, or the environment and start looking around. This can be a big turn off. A good rule of thumb is to maintain eye contact 65 to 70 percent of the time. A technique that may help you to focus on eye contact is counting the other person's blinks. Always try to do more listening than talking, and refrain from looking around when you're in the conversation.

Looking around during a conversation makes you appear distracted and can make the other person feel as though he or she is wasting your time. One of the best ways to avoid this is to maintain eye contact. It makes you appear engaged and interested.

Keep a friendly tone

Your tone does matter. Remember it's not what you say as much as how you say it. Smiling when you talk is a good way to start a conversation.

Don't brag

Avoid stories that focus on your own glory. No one likes to listen to people who talk about themselves too much.

Don't speak to compete

It is easy to hear someone else's story and think you can top it with one of your own, but the fact is, no one cares. Always let the other person be the star of the conversation.

Be careful of jokes

The best type of humor is situational humor or self-deprecating humor. Situational humor is pointing something out within the moment. Doing this can build instant rapport if done correctly. If done incorrectly, it can hurt you instantly. The easiest way to do this is when you start with the OPEN formula. Remember to always stay positive and as you start with the OPEN formula, remember to *react* to your environment, not attack. For example, when you're in attack mode you may say, "Man, that turkey looks so good that (fill in the blank)." That could be a turn-off. However, while in react mode it's much easier to get a laugh. For example, "The turkey must be good, the CEO and I are already on our second plate." Here is a good rule of thumb: If you aren't funny, look to practice with friends and family every chance you get until you get comfortable as humor is a skill that can be learned.

Do - Self-deprecating humor

Self-deprecating humor is making fun of yourself. This is the easiest way to build rapport. For example, if someone asked you about your drive to the event, you can say, "Yes, I live five minutes away but, for some reason I thought I knew a shortcut. I decided to take exit 4 instead of 5. After seven red lights, three McDonald's, and passing the same barking dog four times, I realized I didn't know any shortcuts. It took me thirty minutes to get here. Thirty minutes! I could have walked here in twenty. Needless to say, don't take exit 4 to get here."

> *Self-deprecating humor is making fun of yourself. This is the easiest way to build rapport.*

Do - Drop names

If you meet someone from a different state or someone who works for a company where you know someone, it doesn't hurt to say, "This is a long shot but do you know (fill in the blank)?" If they do know the person, you have just built instant rapport.

Do - Be helpful

Sometimes while you're engaged in a conversation, you may see someone else in the corner of your eye that may be waiting to speak to one of you. If you see this happening just take a step back, open up your body language, and invite her into the conversation.

Do-Pay attention to facial expressions, gestures, and body language

Always pay attention to facial expressions, gestures, and body language. This will give you early signs of whether a person is interested in talking or not. If the person keeps looking around, looking at their watch, or looks bored, then it's time to move on. Keep in mind you're not going to connect with 100 percent of the people you meet.

Do - Help nervous people

When people meet for the first time it is normal to be nervous. The more you use the techniques in this book, the more comfortable you will be with opening a conversation. Sometimes when you start a conversation the other person may be so nervous that they will give short answers. First, you must make sure that this is what is happening. If it is, then ask him a question and throw it back on yourself. For example, you may say:

You: "So, where are you from?"

Contact: "Texas."

You: "Oh, What's the best thing about Texas?"

Contact: "Nothing, really."

You: "Well, I love Texas for three reasons: the people are always nice, the Dallas Cowboys, and the city of San Antonio."

Dealing with negative people

When someone makes a point you don't agree with it's easy to let him know how you feel, but why do that? Try to allow him to save face and instead of disagreeing, give a neutral opinion. Here are some neutral phrases you can say:

1.   That's a thought.

2.   That's one way to look at it.

3. That doesn't work for me, but it could certainly work for someone else.

These types of comments keep you safe from an uncomfortable topic.

The more conversations you start, the more likely it is that you will come across people who always like to be right and battle others.

When someone wants to battle, disagree, or is being rude, you can do the following:

1. Say nothing—This is the safest option.

2. Say, "I'm sure you didn't mean to say it that way?"—This comment will almost certainly get him to think about what he is saying.

Remember, no matter what, always stay positive. Don't feed into negativity.

Activity:

List five do's that stood out to you.

1.

2.

3.

4.

5.

List five don'ts that stood out to you.

1.

2.

3.

4.

5.

Chapter 12

Conversation Killers

"The real art of conversation is not only to say the right thing at the right place but to leave unsaid the wrong thing at the tempting moment."

~Dorothy Nevill

Without a doubt, the fastest way to kill a conversation, lose rapport, or make a bad first impression is being negative. It's amazing how many times I start a conversation with someone and within fifteen seconds, they are complaining, making fun of something, or having a bad day. It's almost like this is the way they try to connect with people.

> *Without a doubt, the fastest way to kill a conversation, lose rapport, or make a bad first impression is being negative.*

Well, if you want to make a good first impression, stay away from making negative comments no matter how enticing it may be. Here are the three most common ways to appear negative:

1. Sarcasm—When people don't know you're being sarcastic you can create miscommunication and appear rude. There is little to gain from being sarcastic, so leave this attitude at home.

2. Complaining—Dale Carnegie once said, "Don't Criticize, Condemn, or Complain." That is powerful advice. No one wants to meet someone who always sees something wrong with everything. Instead, look for things to be positive about and comment on that, and you can't go wrong.

3. Rumors and gossip—Don't gossip by starting a conversation with "Did you know that person (fill in the blank)?"If you gossip, it will seem like you're attracted to drama and like to talk about other people. This is usually a lose-lose situation for you.

Another common way to quickly kill a conversation is to correct someone. No one wants someone they just met ten minutes ago to tell him he is wrong. If they misspeak, let it go. You have more to lose by correcting him than you have to gain. You can instantly lose your connection by making unnecessary corrections.

Here are some examples of what not to say:

1. "Well, it's really (fill in the blank)."

2. "You said (fill in the blank), but it's really (fill in the blank)."

3. "That's not correct."

Don't dominate the conversation. If the conversation is all about you, the other person can quickly lose interest. Try never to talk in more than five-minute intervals. After you talk for a few minutes, check in with the other person by saying, "So, what do you think?" This will keep them engaged.

Stay away from bragging about yourself. No one likes someone who is better than everyone else. Always look to throw in some self-deprecating humor if possible, talk about your lessons learned, and you will be more memorable.

Don't seem too aggressive. Asking back-to-back-to-back questions or playing twenty questions can be intimidating. Use a few good open-ended questions and you should be good to go.

Most of us have heard a great story and think we have a better one to tell. When you do this, you're playing a game called "Top this". When someone tells a great story and you turn around and say, "Well, if you thought that was a great story listen to this…" It can end up being a conversation killer. Use caution with this game. Most people won't appreciate someone they just met topping their story. No matter how amazing your story is, let them remain the superstar by asking questions like:

"That was interesting. How did you (fill in the blank)?"

"What got you (fill in the blank)?"

"When did you (fill in the blank)?"

Don't interrupt others while they are talking. This is the easiest way to bump heads. Try to do more listening than talking. Focus on the conversation at hand, not on what you want to say.

A person who has an answer for everything is a know-it-all. If you have a strong opinion about a subject or know more about a subject than the person talking knows, you can quickly become intimidating and become a turn-off. You don't have to be a know-it-all to be interesting. Listen to his point of view and ask open-ended questions that allow him to appear smarter than you, thus allowing you to build rapport.

> *Don't interrupt others while they are talking. This is the easiest way to bump heads. Try to do more listening than talking.*

Activity:

List five conversation killers that everyone should avoid.

1.

2.

3.

4.

5.

Chapter 13

Getting Out of a Bad Conversation

"Clearly, either side can terminate this agreement."

~Charles Robinson

This is a short chapter, but it contains some powerful tools. Getting out of a conversation can be a challenge for anyone. That's why it's essential to always have a few useful tools to help you escape from any conversation.

It is common to be in a conversation with a really nice person, but when you're ready to move on or need to go somewhere else you just don't know how to end the conversation without appearing rude. This is where the AHEAD technique comes in handy. If you recall the "D"

It is common to be in a conversation with a really nice person, but when you're ready to move on ...

in the AHEAD technique stands for deliver a call to action. By following this technique, you have a road map to exit from virtually any conversation. Believe it or not, as you become a more skilled conversationalist it becomes harder to get out of conversations because more people will like to be in your presence.

Here are some things you can say to terminate a conversation without skipping a beat:

1. "I'm sorry. I have to leave in a few minutes." Then deliver a call to action. You can do this only if you're actually leaving.

2. "I've really enjoyed talking to you Mary, but can you excuse me? I really need to catch Joe before he leaves." In this case, you will need to decide if you want to deliver your call to action now or come back later.

3. "I have to say, I really enjoyed speaking to you. I hope to see you at the next meeting." If you know you're going to run into her soon, you may not need to deliver a call to action.

4. When all else fails you can simply say, "I'm sorry. I need to run to the restroom." Walk away.

Before we go any further, I want to review the technique of delivering a call to action. Delivering a call to action simply means you're giving the other person something to do. Your call to action is meeting up again to ensure you build on what you started.

Here are a few ways to deliver a call to action:

1. "Do you have a business card? I think I may know a few people who could help you."

2. "How does your calendar look for next month? I'd love to discuss that further."

The real key to terminating a conversation is listening. Listening is the key to finding an opening and quickly transitioning out of a conversation. As you're figuring out when you want to terminate a conversation you also need to decide whether you want to keep in contact with that person or not.

To help you along, I encourage you to utilize the LTD technique. This process will help you determine how you want to terminate the conversation. Here are the steps:

1. Listen for an opening—This is the time you're ready to terminate the conversation.

2. Transition out of the conversation— This means you have decided you're

not interested in building a relationship outside this conversation.

3.   Deliver your call to action—This means you are interested in building a relationship outside this conversation.

As we close this chapter it's important to understand these tools are very useful but can backfire in a second if you're not aware of how you choose to exit each conversation. What do I mean? Never forget about your reactions. Always remember the following:

1.   Smile

2.   Keep your energy up

3.   Say their name

Chapter 14

Staying Connected After the First Impression

"We cannot live only for ourselves. A thousand fibers connect us with our fellow men."

~Herman Melville

In this chapter we'll focus on the after-effects of making that great first impression at an event and staying connected to build your network for the future.

Before we go any further, let's discuss one of the most misunderstood terms in business called *networking*. Some people could argue the point that this book is really focused on the art of networking. However, it is really  focused on creating that initial connection with a person. Networking, on the other hand, is the ability to keep those connections after you create them. Many people believe that if they go to an event and meet a bunch of people, they are good networkers. That's just not the case. It's how you stay connected to those people that make you a good networker. That's why this book is critical to your success. You want to ensure you build a strong network and your first impression can lead the way to finding those people who want to stay connected to you.

> *You want to ensure you build a strong network and your first impression can lead the way to finding those people who want to stay connected to you.*

To continually make a good first impression as a business professional, you must assure that you're building a strong network and staying connected.

Here are six quick ways to make sure you stay connected and keep your network alive:

1. Send them a Christmas card. This is a quick and easy way to make them feel guilty because most of us are too busy to take the time to do this. It can go a long way and you only need to do this once a year.

2. Remembering birthdays. An easy way to do this is to ask them without asking.

I learned this techquie from Dale Carnegie. During a conversation, ask them what their zodiac sign is. Once they tell you their sign you can ask them what month is that again and then ask for the day. Of course, you have to do this with excitement. Here's a sample conversation:

You: "What zodiac sign are you?"

Contact: "I'm a Capricorn."

You: Oh... What month is that?"

Contact: "December and January."

You: "I have a friend whose birthday is January 15th. When is yours?"

Contact: "January 5th."

Once you get her birthday, write it down. Send her a birthday card every year. The return on your time investment could be worth millions over your lifetime because she will instantly fall in love with fact someone remembered her birthday.

3. Keep interesting articles that you can send to other people. After I meet someone and find out his interests, I quickly look in my article file and send him something useful that interests him.

4. Always make a note of her causes and immediately follow up. For example: If

she is a dog lover and you know something that can help her, like how to get a discount on dog food or when there is an event for dogs, send that information to her ASAP.

5. Try to connect them with interesting people or with someone who can help them. This isn't being a matchmaker, but it is being a matchmaker. If they like to work on gardens and you know someone else who is an expert in gardens go ahead and formally introduce them through an e-mail, phone call, or in person.

6. Make sure to have enough business cards to hand out and hand them out as needed.

It is fairly common after meeting someone who impressed you to do a Google search on them. Because of this fact it is critical to keep your online identity up to date and current. Today's most popular business social networking site is LinkedIn. It is also a great tool to connect with business professionals and stay connected. I wouldn't discount creating a Facebook account with over one billion users connected to a single social network. Remember, it isn't enough just to create an account, it's just as important to keep them up to date and look to make meaningful connections.

Making a good first impression is critical, but that impression is a starting point. Look to stay connected using the techniques and strategies from this chapter.

This book provides a starting point for creating a great first impression. It is also vital to understand how people view you and how to adapt to different personalities if you're going to be successful at building and keeping your network. I encourage you to visit www.FirstImpressions180.com and take a free assessment.

- Free assessment at www.FirstImpressions180.com.

- Full assessments at www.FirstImpressions180.com.

These personality assessments can help you better understand yourself and others, as well as how to adjust to different personalities to make a great first impression. They can also help you build better relationships in your personal and professional life. I highly recommend checking them out.

Chapter 15

The Three C's of a Business Meeting

*"We bring together the best ideas -
turning the meetings of our top managers
into intellectual orgies."*

~ Jack Welch

Up to this point in the book we've really focused on the social and interactive aspect of the business world, however the majority of time is spent focusing on one thing, the bottom line.

Business meetings are a broad category. Most business professionals have customer meetings on a daily, weekly, or monthly basis. For the discussion in this book we will focus on the initial meeting with a new customer. This can be very intimidating as you are

This can be very intimidating as you are being judged in most cases based on the opinion and past experiences of the customer.

being judged in most cases based on the opinion and past experiences of the customer. Although you can't change how a customer views perspective business partners, you can minimize negative views. It goes without saying your appearance can be significant for a first impression. Please review Chapter 10 for tricks, tips, and techniques when dealing with your appearance.

In this chapter we'll explore the three C's of business meetings.

The first C stands for command of the facts. This is by far the most important aspect of a business meeting. There are countless stories of business meetings gone wrong because someone wasn't prepared for the meeting.

This concept was introduced to me during one of the rougher business experiences of my life. It was the first time I was brought on to run a multimillion dollar project by myself. I wasn't briefed on the project by my team, I wasn't familiar with the technology, I didn't know the processes for the customer, I didn't know anyone on the project, needless to say it was like being thrown in the middle of the ocean and being asked to find land for the first few weeks. In my first meeting I didn't know what to expect. I decided to keep a low profile and just observe the customer and the other managers interact. When I was introduced to the customer as the new project manager they immediately picked up on the fact I was so quiet and asked me when I thought the completion date would be. With a blank look in my eyes and seven long seconds of silence a manager named Sidney McCall spoke up and said "June 15th." If you ever met Sid you would quickly realize this is a person that has had very few enemies in his life. After the meeting, he sat down with me and explained how everything was structured and the expectations of the customer. He said, "If you want to survive with this customer you need to make sure you always have command of the facts at every meeting or they will eat you alive." From that initial meeting it took me months to gain the trust of the customer. Looking back that was one of the most important pieces of advice I ever received in my career and was a direct factor of me being successful within that project and being successful within every other project I lead moving forward.

Looking back that was one of the most important pieces of advice I ever received in my career...

Command of the facts is by far, in my opinion, the most important tool you can have entering into any meeting. If you can't remember all of them then make sure you have them close by, maybe in your back up slides. Learn from my mistake, before going into an initial customer meeting ensure you have command of the facts. Here are a few things you can do to reassure you have command of the facts from day 1.

- Understand the organizations structure.

- Understand their processes or how they do business.

- Research your department and mission.

- Ask coworkers how things are run and what to expect.

When you have command of the facts it ultimately allows you to do two key things, anticipate and minimize. It will allow you to anticipate and prepare for what may be asked. This will allow you to prepare for the meeting in a very effective matter.

Secondly, you can minimize what you're going to say to ensure you don't ramble on and provide clear concise answers. Those two aspects of command of the facts feed directly into the second C.

Nothing has more conviction in a business meeting than asking a question and having the feeling this person is an expert in the field.

The second C stands for Confidence. Nothing has more conviction in a business meeting than asking a question and having the feeling this person is an expert in the field with their answer. Sometimes the person will have command of the facts and sometimes they won't but if the customer is at ease from the beginning based on what they see, hear, and feel it may not matter. This is where perception vs. reality can play a part in a successful meeting. If the customer perceives you're an expert on the topic and you carry yourself in that manner you may be able to fake it until you make it. Make no mistake about it, one successful meeting doesn't mean much if you bomb the next time. If you're lucky that first meeting, make certain you have command of the facts moving forward.

When I started to present on a daily basis to the customer they would question every fact and figure I presented stemming from that first meeting. My management team asked an experienced program manager named Kevin Thibeault (pronounced like Kevin Tebow) to review my project and determine if I was getting the job done. If you ever met Kevin you would quickly realize he is a no nonsense, get it done type of guy. After sitting down with me and reviewing my work he said "From everything I see your doing an excellent job." It was the first time in months I felt good about what I was doing. He said "We are going to do two things. Number one; we are going to give them so much data in your morning presentation they will stop questioning your every word you say and two; you're going to present with confidence." Confidence within a business meeting puts everyone at ease and makes you appear to be an expert. Within a few weeks my charts answered all questions and my confidence rose 200 percent within days. My presentations moving forward were about building trust and effective relationships with the customer and fortunately I've never had any real issue I couldn't handle on the fly again.

Here are the key things I've learned that can help you appear more confident in your next meeting:

- Voice – Speak with conviction.

- Eye contact – Make sure you look whoever you're talking to directly in the eye.

- Answers – Make certain you answer all questions with confidence and conviction.

- Listen – Ensure you utilize time active listening discussed in Chapter 8.

- Questions – Make sure you ask meaningful questions.

I'll make the point once more, although confidence may get you past the first meeting, I highly recommend you enter into all future meetings with command of the facts as they will catch up to you sooner rather than later.

The final C stands for Conscious. This is a lesson one of my managers Hector Hernandez ingrained into my head with every meeting we prepared for. Hector is the type of person that thinks three steps ahead before speaking and was a great

"You need to be conscious about what the customer says with their words, their body, and their answers."

mentor. He would often say to me, "You need to be conscious about what the customer says with their words, their body, and their answers." When a business meeting starts it's paramount that you stay conscious of your customers. The customer will possibly give clues as to how they feel the meeting is going. It's up to you to pick up on these small clues and build on them.

- Did I ask the right questions?
- What does their body language say?
- Do they look interested?
- Do they look bored?
- Do I need to change direction?
- Do they believe what I'm saying?
- Are they interested in something else?

Once you start focusing on these clues you can guide the meeting down the path you want and start to make adjustments when you deem necessary or build on the momentum that has already been built.

Before we end this chapter it's worth mentioning practice facilitating a meeting. One of the best places to practice this skill as well as learning how to keep a meeting on schedule is Toastmasters International. Every meeting has a facilitator.

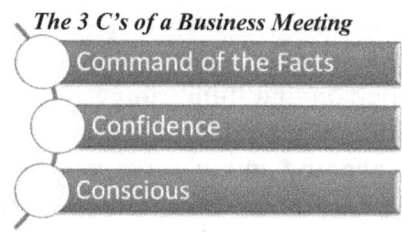

The 3 C's of a Business Meeting

Command of the Facts

Confidence

Conscious

This job teaches you how to put an agenda together, make sure all key sections are coordinated, and make certain the meeting stays on track and on time. You also get an opportunity to observe different styles as you fine tune your own style. I highly recommend finding a local Toastmasters club near you by visiting www.toastmasters.org.

Review:

What are the 3 C's of a business meeting?

1.

2.

3.

Provide 3 examples of the first C.

1.

2.

3.

Provide 3 examples of the second C.

1.

2.

3.

Provide 3 examples of the third C.

1.

2.

3.

Chapter 16

Start Your Presentation with a Bang

"It takes one hour of preparation for each
minute of presentation time."

~ Wayne Burgraff

There are many books written on the topic of
presentations. This chapter isn't intended to replace
them but provide you with some strategies for
presenting to new business clients. As you go into a
business presentation with a potential client your
presentation will determine if you get the account or
not and every second counts so it's imperative to
ensure you start, stay, and finish on the right track
during your presentation.

We are assuming you're new to the
presentation world and if you're not hopefully this
chapter will provide you with a few more tools
you can add to your tool belt. We recommend the
best way to get started is taking a step back and
studying someone else's presentation.

A few great shows to watch and study on this topic are *Shark Tank* and *The Pitch*. These shows are focused on that initial business presentation to win business. Let's take a deeper look into each show.

The Pitch is a reality show from AMC that goes behind the scenes with two different ad agencies each week competing to win a new marketing account. Initially, both agencies meet the client at the same time for an initial meeting to capture the task at hand. What's interesting in this meeting is very few questions are asked, because one agency doesn't want to give the other agency an advantage. Then for the next seven days you get a front row seat into the creative process of two companies putting a marketing campaign together for the potential client. The second part is the "*The Pitch*", which is a presentation that brings each agencies idea to life. The final piece belongs to the client as they select a winner based on who they felt captured their vision the best. You get to observe who hit the mark and who didn't. A lot of times one agency did well in certain areas and the other agency did well in other areas. Each episode provides insight into outstanding presentations.

Shark Tank is another reality show with a focus on entrepreneurs pitching their business or product to five wealthy investors called "Sharks." The goal is for the entrepreneur to offer a percentage of the business and in return the Shark will provide funding, expertise, and their network.

If you study the show carefully the most successful entrepreneurs use the three C's of any business meeting discussed in the last chapter.

With either one of these shows every presentation is around five minutes long with potentially millions on the line. That means your first impression is all you have during the presentation. That means there is only one way to think about your first impression, it could be worth millions of dollars.

That means there is only one way to think about your first impression, it could be worth millions of dollars.

One of the most important aspects of your presentation is *knowing your audience*. In *The Pitch* the ad agencies actually have an initial meeting to determine what the assignment is and ask questions to fine tune their focus. Prior to that initial meeting each ad agency goes even further by researching things like what the company is about, who is the executive team, what is the company culture, past performance of the company, and anything else that may give them an advantage ahead of time. *Shark Tank* has a different formula for *knowing your audience* as each entrepreneur presenting needs to know which shark would be the best investor, who has the expertise to get them to the next level, how they became rich, and even their successes and failures in order to frame their presentation to make an emotional connection as quickly as possible. Before going into any initial business presentation ensure you know the audience and look to make a connection as quickly as possible.

The second focus of your presentation should be *getting to the point*. Think about it in terms of a commercial. Companies spend millions of dollars for a 30 second slot. A commercial's sole objective is to grab your attention instantly and get you to want to buy their product or service within 30 seconds. Now you'll probably have more than 30 seconds but the potential client will want to know what the presentation is about as soon as possible. This can be a challenge because you may need to present an essential back story with details that explain the product or service but you don't want to bore them to death. A great way to balance this need is to create a tagline for the product or service. Verizon has a great tagline *"Can you hear me now?"* for cell phone service. 99% of cell users have asked that question when service has been temporarily interrupted and any time I ask that question today I automatically think about Verizon. Imagine starting your presentation with are you tired of saying *"Can you hear me now."* Welcome to the only cell phone carrier that covers 99.99% of the world for one low price. This is getting to the point. You are providing a solution for dead calls at one low price. The client will know exactly where the presentation is going and allow you to provide a back story and details if needed.

The third area to focus on is making sure you *never lose your audience.* To ensure your presentation has the right mix of elements while confirming no one is lost during the presentation it is recommended that you practice and test it out in front of a few different audiences. Feedback is critical and you should listen to everyone. If people keep asking the same questions make sure your presentation answers them. A critical piece of advice we can give you is never fall in love with your presentation until others provide feedback.

The final piece of this framework is *close with the bottom line.* If you're presenting to an investor you may say "We're looking for a $250,000 dollar investment for 10% of the company." Using the Verizon example earlier you could add a reference to your tagline in the closing by saying "With the help of your $250,000 dollar investment for 10% of the company together we will eliminate the phrase, "Can you hear me now?" in the cell phone industry. Along with closing with the bottom line you and your team should anticipate possible questions after the presentation so be prepared.

As you start giving presentations it's essential to practice as much as possible. The best place to practice presentation skills is again one of your local Toastmasters clubs. Toastmasters gives you a positive environment to practice speeches at all levels. They provide speech projects that allow you to practice in all major areas of public speaking (speech structure, vocal variety, delivery, etc.) and most importantly after every speech you are provided feedback. Feedback is something you rarely receive after a business presentation, but without it getting better or breaking bad habits can become difficult.

Another useful tool Toastmasters provides is speaking competitions. I was once told by a seasoned Toastmaster John Melmed "The fastest way to become a great speaker or presenter is to enter a competition." This is an opportunity to benchmark your skills against the best in the world.

Toastmasters has a flagship competition called the International Speech Contest. This annual contest hosts over 35,000 speakers worldwide competing for the crown of *World Champion of Public Speaking*. In 2009, I finished within the top 20 in the world. Although, I didn't win the title, the experience within the competition was priceless.

While self-paced speaking projects and contests are great tools, in my opinion, the most beneficial skill Toastmasters helps you work on are your impromptu speaking skills for the business world. Few things are more difficult in the business world than having to improvise on the fly within a customer meeting. Toastmasters actually allows you to practice this skill at each meeting with something called Table Topics. During this portion of the meeting the host will ask random questions to people and they have 1 – 2 minutes to answer the question. The first time I was asked one of these random questions I got so nervous my

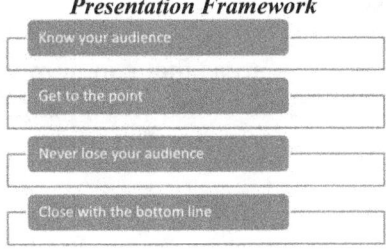

Presentation Framework

Know your audience

Get to the point

Never lose your audience

Close with the bottom line

mind went blank and I lasted a whole 15 seconds. In a business meeting thinking on your feet is a critical skill that should be practiced as much as possible.

From a business prospective Table Topic's teach you three critical skills.

1. Buying time – Whenever you're asked a question and you need a couple extra seconds to think about it, ask them to repeat it.

2. Understanding the question – If you're not sure paraphrase it to make sure everyone is on the same page. You can start by saying "If I understand you, I think what you're saying…"

3. Practice – These questions challenge you mentally and allow you to test your skills in front of strangers.

Review:

List the 4 areas that can help you start and finish your presentation with a bang:

1.

2.

3.

4.

What is a tagline and how can it help you in your next presentation?

Why should you always have command of the facts during your presentation?

Chapter 17

How to be a STAR in Any Interview

"The best interviews -- like the best biographies -- should sing the strangeness and variety of the human race."

~ Lynn Barber

An interview can be one of the more challenging experience's you have as a business professional. Many times they will determine a promotion, a new career path, or a career change which largely depends on your first and only impression. There are hundreds of books written on this topic, as a matter of fact, amazon.com currently has over 6,000 books on the topic of interview skills.

An interview can be one of the more challenging experience's you have as a business professional.

Really your first impression in an interview starts with your resume. Since we aren't going to cover your resume in detail it is highly recommended you work with a professional. A few things you should be aware of:

1. Most resumes are scanned for key words so make sure your resume has the key words associated with the job you are applying for prior to sending it out.

2. Review for spelling and grammar errors.

3. Finalize your resume by ensuring each section highlights your talents.

Having a strong network could be the single most influential tool you have to getting that dream job.

A key area before the resume stage is verifying if anyone in your network is connected to the job you're applying for. Underutilizing this aspect is how people are passed over and why it's critical that you stay in touch with as many people as possible in your network. Prior to submitting your resume you should review your rolodex. Look to see if you know someone or know someone who may know someone that works for the company you're interviewing with. Having a strong network could be the single most influential tool you have to getting that dream job.

Remember, never discount a conversation and always look to make a great first impression when building your network at all times.

I have extensive experience in interviews. As a graduate of a 3 year Fortune 500 Leadership Development Program, I had 12 interviews within a 3 year time span. We would work on different assignments within the company which could span anywhere between 3 – 6 months at a time. Each time I went to a new assignment I had to interview for it as others where competing for it as well. I would say I learned more on the interviews I failed because I would go back and analyze what I could have improved on. At the end of this chapter I'll discuss how I got my dream job after I graduated my program. The amazing thing was I was interviewing for a completely different job.

Ok, once you get that call to be interviewed it's time to start preparing.

Have answers prepared for the following questions about yourself:

1. Tell me a little about yourself? Here's an example to get you started: I grew up on the north side of Chicago. On that side of town you have no choice but to be a Cubs fan so I'm used to disappointment in my life (Any baseball fan knows this is a joke referring to the Cubs not winning a championship in over 100 years). After high school…

2. Where do you want to be in five years? This takes some planning but you want the interviewer to know you know where you want to go in life.

3. Tell me a little about your last job. This needs to be thought out. It is one of the most overlooked and least prepared for questions people answer mainly because they fail to uncover the many critical things they do on a daily, weekly, monthly, and yearly basis.

4. Why are you looking for a new job? Your answers should always be positive. For example: "I'm looking for a new challenge," or "I'm looking for a career change."

5. Tell me a weakness you have. Again, be positive. For example: "Sometimes I need to learn to take a break because I get so focused on the task itself..."

These are what I consider warm up questions and you should always be prepared to answer them. You can probably find 50 - 100 other warm up questions on the internet but the questions above always seem to be standard for me.

The next area you should be prepared for are field and role related questions.

1. Are you familiar with X software?

2. What roles and responsibilities did you have at your last job?

The third area, which is the hardest area of an interview, is situational based questions. For this area I recommend using the STAR Method.

The STAR method is a framework for dealing with behavior based questions by outlining the situation or task reviewing the action you took and closing the result. Let's take a closer look.

Situation: You're looking to paint a picture of the actual situation that is asked. Make sure you're as specific as possible about the event providing enough detail to make the interviewer feel they are with you.

Task: Look to frame the situation with a specific goal or task that you are looking to accomplish.

Action: At this point, you're looking to convey the action YOU took to address the situation. Look to walk them through the specific step you took.

Result: Describe the end result of how you succeeded. What was your key take away? Remember to tell a story and make a point. What did you accomplish?

Sample question and response:

Tell me a time in your business career that you dealt with failure and how you overcame it?

Situation/Task: It was my second day of work. I was so excited to start work I left home 30 minutes earlier than I needed to. I was about half way to work when my car started to sputter. I just wanted to get to the shoulder before my car shutdown in the middle of the highway. As I coasted over to the shoulder I realized I had run out of gas. I couldn't believe it! I left earlier to guarantee I would be early for my first meeting and now I was staring down the possibility of missing a half day of work.

Action: As I sat in the car trying to figure out a way to make the meeting it dawned on me to dial in. I called the lobby and got the number.

Result: I was so embarrassed about running out of gas that I told everyone I got a flat tire as I introduced myself. Everyone on the team was amazed I went through all that trouble the second day on the job and I was given the nickname "Mr. Dependable."

Earlier I told you I received a dream job offer as I was interviewing for a totally different job.

When I graduated from my Leadership Development Program I had to find a new job within the company. I reached out to my network and one of my old managers ended up getting me an interview for a management job because of what I did for him a few years back. This really wasn't the job I wanted but at the time jobs were scarce so it was better to take an offer than try to find the perfect job and end up with nothing. The interview started off smooth with a panel of 3 interviewers asking a few warm up questions. Then the technical questions started and after five questions they knew my technical knowledge wasn't there for this position. One of the interviewers asked me, "What do you really want to do within the next five years?" For the next 45 minutes we talked about technical questions in that field, situational questions on how I could help the program, and where I really wanted to be in five years. They offered me the job and a promotion on the spot. I was once told "it's better to be prepared and not have an opportunity than have an opportunity and not be prepared." Even though I prepared to interview for a different job I was always prepared to talk about my five year plan and it worked out perfectly within that moment.

Review:

Why is your resume so important for an interview?

List 3 things you should do prior to submitting your resume:

1.

2.

3.

List three warm up interview questions that you should be prepared to answer:

1.

2.

3.

How should you prepare for the technical portion of your interview?

What does STAR stand for?

S

T

A

R

What type of questions does STAR help you prepare for?

Tips for preparing for your STAR interview:

- List 10 situation's in your career that taught you a lesson.

- They don't have to be significant situations, just stories that can teach everyone a lesson.

- Frame each initial situation so everyone can follow you easily.

- Each story has a beginning, middle, end, and a point.

- Each story reflects a point or lesson that is favorable.

- Each story is specific with enough detail to account for each event.

- Make sure to have a variety of stories covering different situations in your life and your career.

Sample behavior based questions:

1. Tell me a time you had to overcome a failure.

2. How do you handle challenges in the work place? Give an example.

3. Have you ever made a mistake? How did you handle it?

4. Describe a decision you made that wasn't popular and how you handled implementing it?

5. Give an example of a goal you reached and tell me how you reached it?

Chapter 18

First Impressions
When You're Not in Person

*"First impressions count,
even when they're not in person."*

~Anonymous

First impressions consume our professional careers on a daily basis on both sides (what we perceive and how other's perceive us).
Most times we focus on the personal interaction side of first impressions to ensure we make a good impression with most of the people we interact with on a daily basis. As business professionals we are always looking to hit deadlines, meet goals, and deliver results. It is during this time we can get extremely busy and overlook the importance of email and phone call etiquette that

> *Most times we focus on the personal interaction side of first impressions to ensure ...*

could help guarantee you meet your next deadline while making a great first impression.

When you enter into the work environment email is a critical tool that is extremely important to your success. Due to the fact words can be interpreted many different ways it is up to you to ensure your emails are clear, concise, and positive at all times.

Before we go into email etiquette make sure you have a professional offline or private email account to handle business related matters. If you have something like oneeyewillie567@yahoo.com please create a new account that shows you're professional. First and last name is fine.

Let's take a look at the subject heading line. The end result of your subject is to make certain the receiver opens it. Here are a few tips when constructing your next subject heading.

1. It should be short and relevant

2. Eye catching

3. Intriguing

Here are a few examples:

1. The final piece to your report

2. Question: Final meeting with X customer

3. Don't be the last to submit

All three examples are teases into something the receiver needs. As a business professional it is pretty common to get a100 emails a day. Most people will skim to find important ones and the others are forgotten. With a powerful subject that teases the reader you can almost always be sure your email will be opened.

Salutation: The greeting is essential as you start your email. There are hundreds of articles that can give you different rules of thumb. The simplest rule of thumb is to start off by stating Dear Mr. X or Dear Ms. Y. In this situation you always show respect.

Body: Within the body of your email you should always look to have a positive tone that addresses the need within the email. No one wants to read a book so make sure your body is clear, concise, positive, but to the point. Personally, I like to use bullet point to outline my major points if needed.

Closing: As you close your email make certain your bottom line is clear. Lastly, you should use a closing line. Here are a few that should do the trick.
Sincerely

1.   Thanks for your support

2.   If you need anything please let me know

Signature: Your signature should be used so people know who you are and how to contact you. Here's an example:

Name
Company
Position
Address

Phone
Fax

Now, let's switch gears to the phone calls.
During the heat of a
deadline you may not
know everyone you talk to
however you should
always remain positive and
helpful with every phone
call.

*By far your tone
is the most
important aspect
as the
conversation...*

Below are some tips,
tricks, and techniques for phone calls.

1. Tone: By far your tone is the most
    important aspect as the conversation is
    initiated. Make sure to answer the
    phone being friendly, open, and genuine
    no matter what you have going on.

2. Rate: Make sure you speak slowly and
    clearly as you answer the phone. This
    should create a calm mood throughout
    the conversation.

3. Positive: Look to comment on the
    positive side of the situation and speak
    with a smile. Speaking with a smile
    subconsciously keeps you in a positive
    mood.

4. Focused: You should stop what you're
    doing and focus on the conversation at
    hand. Nothing is more annoying than to

hear typing in the background and having to repeat yourself because the other person isn't paying attention.

5. Never eat: Stay away from snacking, chewing gum, or sucking on candy.

6. Listening: Be a better listener than a talker. Don't interrupt and look to take notes.

7. End the conversation: End the conversation by thanking them.

8. Follow up with an email to ensure you have a record of the call if the conversation was important.

Review:

Email

List three attributes a good subject line should have:

1.

2.

3.

What is the simplest rule of thumb for starting off your salutation?

What type of tone should the body of your email always have?

List three ways you can close your email:

1.

2.

3.

What are the six key elements of an email signature?

1.

2

3.

4.

5.

6.

Phone Calls

List qualities your tone should have every time you answer the phone:

1.

2.

3.

Why should you always try to speak slow and clear?

Why is it so important to stay focused on the caller?

How should you follow up with important phone calls?

Readers Guide

NSP (Negative Self-Phrase) – Common phrases we use to tell ourselves that something negative will happen.

Key: When you find yourself using NSP's remember nothing good ever comes from negative thoughts. Positive thinking will only bring positive results.

PSP (Positive Self-Phrase) – Common phrases we use to tell ourselves that something positive will happen.

Key: This is your mental golden ticket to ensure positive things will happen.

AHEAD Technique

- **A**ttention grabber—Create an opening statement that will stimulate curiosity and cause intrigue about yourself.

- **H**ave a benefit (to your target point, e.g., company or job)—Share an interesting experience you gained from your job.

- **E**ngage with a story—Entice with an interesting story.

- **A**lways seek to make a connection—Put the focus back on him and try to connect with him.

- **D**eliver a call to action—Seek to connect with her at a later date.

Key: Make yourself memorable in 15 seconds or less and then build on it.

LTD Technique

- **L**isten for an opening—This is the time you're ready to terminate the conversation.

- **T**ransition out of the conversation—This means you have decided you're not interested in building a relationship outside this conversation.

- **D**eliver your call to action—This means you are interested in building a relationship outside this conversation.

OPEN formula

- **O**bserve your environment.

- **P**osition to listen.

- **E**xplore for more.

- **N**ever neglect yourself.

Key: Start and keep a conversation going with ease.

R-SMARTS

- **R**educe negative snap judgments—Reduce how others perceive you negatively.

- **S**OFTEN them up—Minimize your bad habits.

- **M**irror their movement—Synchronize yourself with the other person.

- **A**lways remember names—Pay attention when someone tells you their name.

- **R**emain positive—Always appear positive.

- **T**ime active listening—Actively listen for key wants and needs.

- **S**hare the workload—Reciprocate actions.

Key: Build rapport within minutes and keep it.

SOFTEN Technique

- **S**mile—Remember to smile once a minute.

- **O**pen posture—Stand with confidence and allow your body to be open and inviting.

- **F**orward lean—Lean forward to show interest in the conversation.

- **T**one of voice—Speak in a calm and unhurried tone of voice.

- **E**ye contact—Try to make eye contact 70 to 80 percent of the time.

- **N**od head–Nodding your head shows that you're interested in the conversation.

Key: Keep your body language positive at all times

STAR Method

- **S**ituation—You're looking to paint a picture of the actual situation that is asked. Make sure you're as specific as possible about the event providing enough detail to make the interviewer feel they are with you.

- **T**ask— Frame the situation with a specific goal or task that you were looking to accomplish.

- **A**ction— At this point you're looking to convey the action YOU took to address the situation. Walk them through the specific steps you took.

- **R**esult—Describe the end result of how you succeeded. What was your key take away? Remember, tell a story make a point. What did you accomplish?

Key: Used in situational based interviewing questions.

Final Thought

Congratulations, you've finished the book and now it's time to start a new journey in your life. I recommend reviewing your activities weekly and practicing these tools, techniques, and strategies on a daily basis. The more you work on them the faster they will become second nature to you. As you master this book, you won't have to look for opportunities because opportunities will find you.

I wish you the best of luck in the future and hope this book will help make a difference in your life and in the lives of the people around you. You now have the power to always make yourself memorable in any situation with a great first impression.

www.ingramcontent.com/pod-product-compliance
Lightning Source LLC
Chambersburg PA
CBHW051507170526
45166CB00001B/420